Skills

Problem Solving and Reasoning

Karen Morrison
Lisa Greenstein

OXFORD

Great Clarendon Street, Oxford, OX2 6DP, United Kingdom

Oxford University Press is a department of the University of Oxford. It furthers the University's objective of excellence in research, scholarship, and education by publishing worldwide. Oxford is a registered trade mark of Oxford University Press in the UK and in certain other countries.

© Cloud Publishing and Lisa Greenstein Publishing 2024

The moral rights of the authors have been asserted

First published in 2024

All rights reserved. No part of this publication may be reproduced, stored in a retrieval system, or transmitted, in any form or by any means, without the prior permission in writing of Oxford University Press, or as expressly permitted by law, by licence or under terms agreed with the appropriate reprographics rights organization. Enquiries concerning reproduction outside the scope of the above should be sent to the Rights Department, Oxford University Press, at the address above.

You must not circulate this work in any other form and you must impose this same condition on any acquirer

British Library Cataloguing in Publication Data
Data available

9781382044523

10 9 8 7 6 5 4 3 2 1

The manufacturing process conforms to the environmental regulations of the country of origin.

Printed in China by Golden Cup

Acknowledgements
The publisher and authors would like to thank the following for permission to use photographs and other copyright material:

Photos: p13: mariakray / Shutterstock; **p20:** Kletr / Shutterstock; **p25:** Mike Richter / Shutterstock; **p26:** BlueRingMedia / Shutterstock; **p32:** Kletr / Shutterstock; **p34:** M. Unal Ozmen / Shutterstock; **p35:** redmal / E+ / Getty Images; **p38(a):** BMCL / Shutterstock; **p38(b):** Elnur / 123 RF; **p38(c):** Nadia Cruzova / Shutterstock; **p38(d):** Larisa Lofitskaya / Shutterstock; **p38(e):** ratmaner / 123 RF; **p38(f):** Studio KIWI / Shutterstock; **p46(a), 47:** Lightspring / Shutterstock; **p46(b, c, d):** Daria Riabets / Shutterstock; **p56(t):** Elena Masiutkina / Shutterstock; **p56(b):** JIANG HONGYAN / Shutterstock; **p57:** belchonock / 123RF; **p59:** Nataly Studio / Shutterstock; **p61:** PeterVrabel / Shutterstock; **p62:** Elena Elisseeva / Shutterstock; **p66:** robbylokamp / Shutterstock; **p68(a):** Visun Khankasem / Shutterstock; **p68(b):** Gareth Dewar / Alamy Stock Photo; **p68(c):** Photojulia / Shutterstock; **p68(d):** Timothy Roesdiah / Shutterstock; **p71(a):** Jim Barber / Shutterstock; **p71(b):** NIKCOA / Shutterstock; **p71(c):** Cuson / Shutterstock; **p71(d):** Yarygin / Shutterstock; **p71(e):** Andy Piatt / Shutterstock; **p71(f):** YJ.K / Shutterstock; **p71(g):** Tanya Gracheva / Shutterstock; **p71(h):** Stanko / Shutterstock; **p71(i):** Vladimir Arndt / Shutterstock; **p75:** Andrey Emelyanenko / Shutterstock.

Cover art: Andrea Manzati.

Artwork by: Katya Balakina, Q2A Media, James Elston and Oxford University Press.

Every effort has been made to contact copyright holders of material reproduced in this book. Any omissions will be rectified in subsequent printings if notice is given to the publisher.

Contents

My problem-solving record 4

1 Neighbours 6
Along the street 6
Counting windows 8
Mixing paint 10
Playing around 12
Who lives there? 14
Sharing with our neighbours 16

2 Trees and forests 18
Measuring trees 18
The tallest trees in the world 20
How old is that tree? 22
Planting trees 24
In the rainforest 26
Map it out 28

3 Let's go shopping 30
At the shops 30
At the flower stall 32
The ice cream shop 34
Packaging problems 36
It's on sale 38
Check your change 40

4 Sports day 42
Counting cones 42
The 100 m race 44
Basketball hoops 46
The egg-and-spoon race 48
The obstacle race 50
Keeping time 52

5 Growing plants 54
Planting a bean 54
Using seed trays 56
Seeds and rows 58
Choosing what to plant 60
Plants need water 62
Measuring in the garden 64

6 Exploring patterns and shapes 66
Mosaics 66
Square patterns 68
Circles and other round shapes 70
Decorate the cakes 72
Number patterns 74
Symmetrical patterns 76

Glossary 78

My problem-solving record

These are the steps I follow to solve a problem…

1 Read and understand the problem → **2** Choose a strategy

These are the strategies I tried…

Act out the problem
1 2 3 4 5 6

Use objects to model the problem
1 2 3 4 5 6

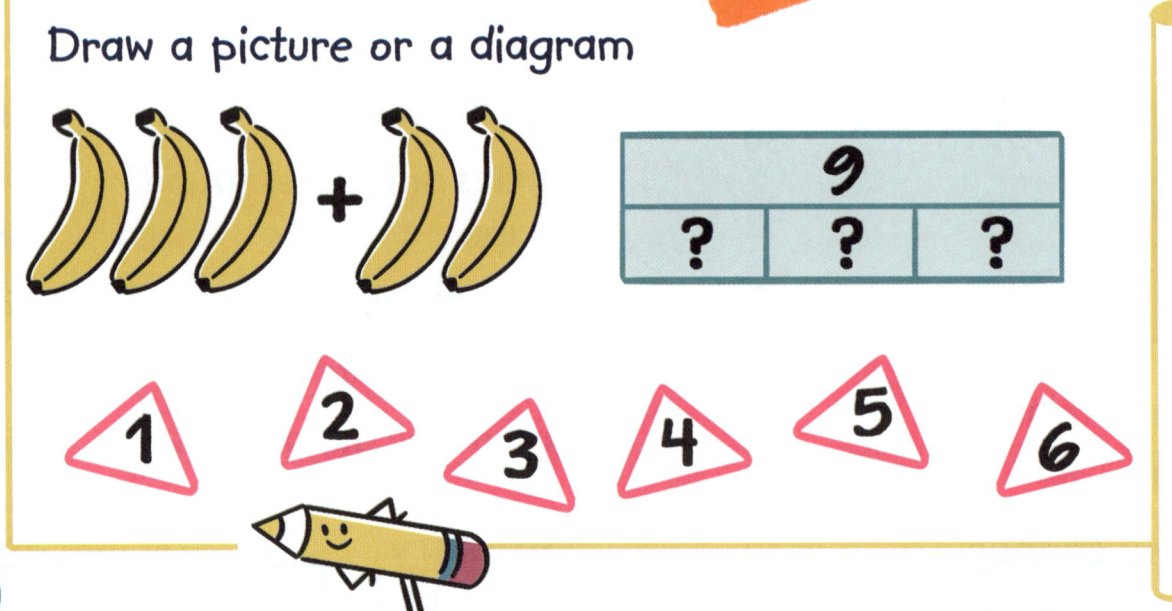

Draw a picture or a diagram
1 2 3 4 5 6

3 Work out the solution
- do maths
- show your work

4 Check your answers
- compare with a partner

Look for patterns and make connections

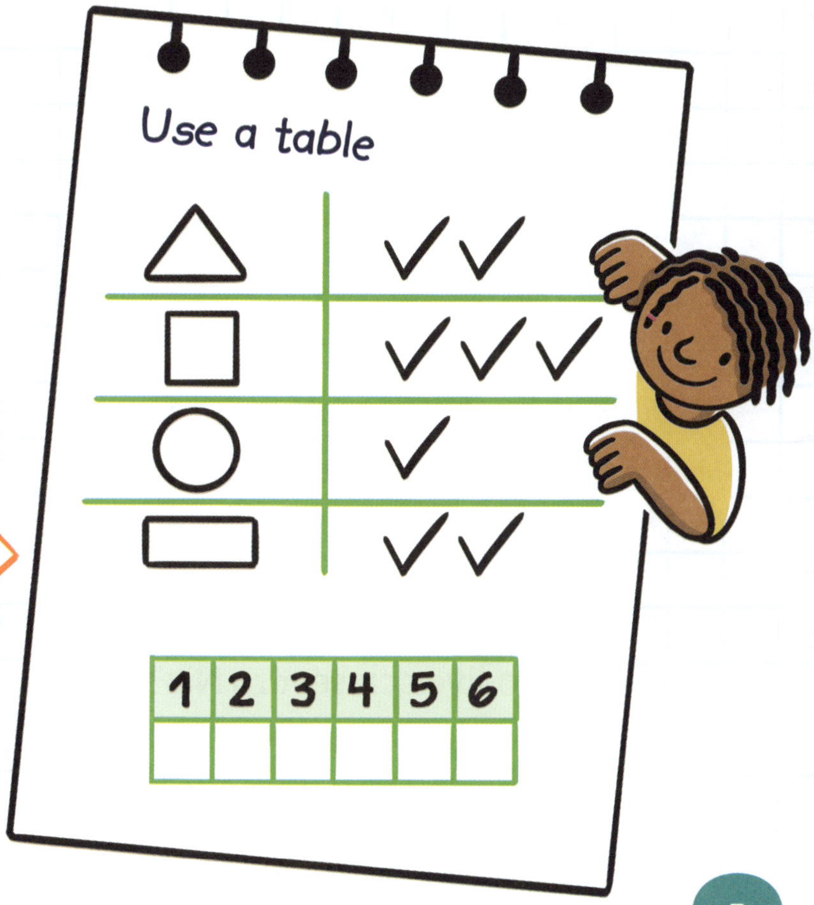

2 → 4 → 6 → 8...   COUNT 2s

NEXT SHAPE IS ▨

1	2
3	4
5	6

Make a list

2 ▲ s
3 ◼ s
1 ● s
2 ▬ s

| ✓ |
| 1 |
| 2 |
| 3 |
| 4 |
| 5 |
| 6 |

Use a table

△	✓✓
◻	✓✓✓
○	✓
▭	✓✓

| 1 | 2 | 3 | 4 | 5 | 6 |
| | | | | | |

1 Neighbours

Let's reason …

All the houses on Miri's side of the street have **even numbers**.
Miri's address is 4 Long Street.

1. Finn's house has rooms upstairs and downstairs.

   Finn's house number is less than Miri's house number.

   What is his house number? _____

2. Nandi lives on the other side of Miri. What is Nandi's address?

   _____

3. On the other side of Long Street, the houses have **odd numbers**.
   Kofi lives at number 15. Nic lives at number 5.
   Joy lives at number 51. Mercy lives at number 25.

   Circle the correct name.

   a. Who lives closest to Nic's house?   Kofi   Mercy

   b. Who lives between Nic and Mercy?   Joy   Kofi

   c. Who lives furthest from Mercy's house?   Nic   Joy

Along the street

Think, talk, write

4 These house numbers are all from the same street.
The odd-numbered houses are on one side of the street.
The even-numbered houses are on the other side.

- Sort the house numbers according to the side of the street they are on.
- Write the numbers in order from lowest to highest.

Odd numbers						
Even numbers						

5 Four cars are parked in the street.

a Read the clues and colour the cars correctly.

> Read all the clues before you start.

Finn's car is blue. It is not parked in front of Mai's house.

Li's car is green. It is parked in front of number 16.

Jo's car is yellow.

Mai lives at number 14. Her car is black. It is parked in front of her neighbour's house.

b How did you work out which car belongs to each person? Tell your partner.

7

Let's reason ...

1 Read how some students counted the windows on this house.

I counted the windows one by one.

I skip counted in twos.

I counted groups and added.

I counted in fives.

Which way of counting do you like best?
Why do you like it? Tell your partner.

2 Find two different ways to count the windows on each apartment block. Tell your partner how you counted.

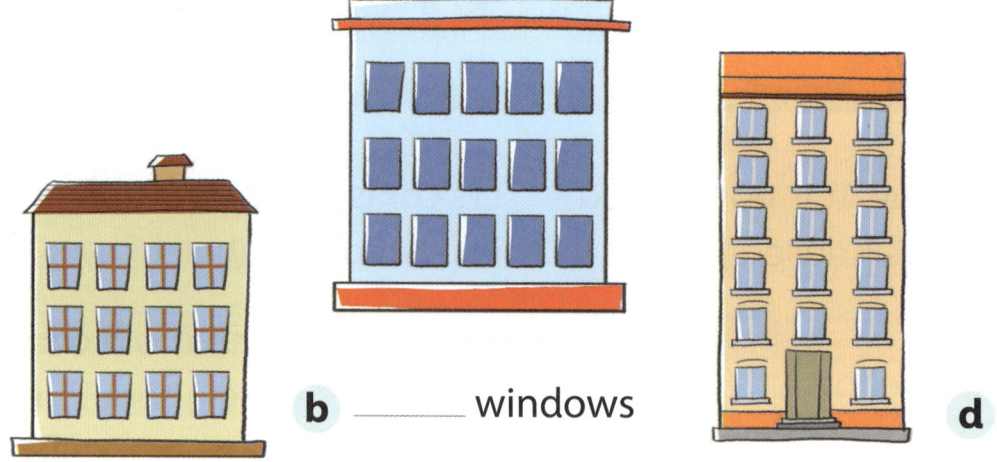

a _____ windows

b _____ windows

c _____ windows

d _____ windows

Counting windows

Think, talk, write

Bar models can help us solve problems.

I count 6 windows on Block A and 5 windows on Block B. How many windows do I count?

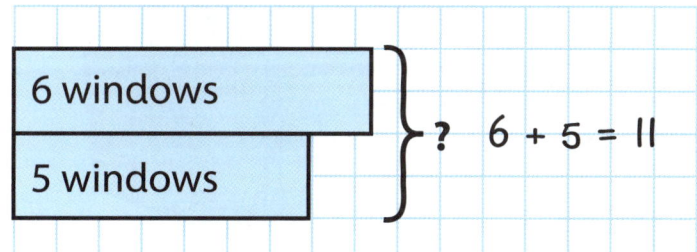

3 Work with a partner. Make up a problem to match each bar model. Write a number sentence. Solve it and write the answer.

> Look carefully at each bar model. Do you need to add, subtract or halve the numbers?

a
- 5 windows
- 5 windows
- 2 windows
- ?

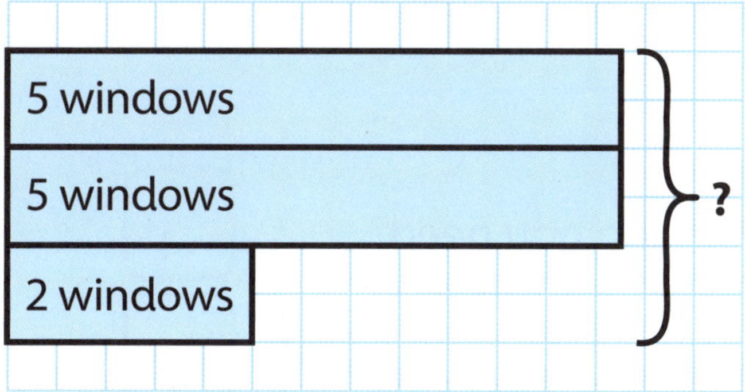

b
- Block A 12 windows
- Block B 9 windows
- ?

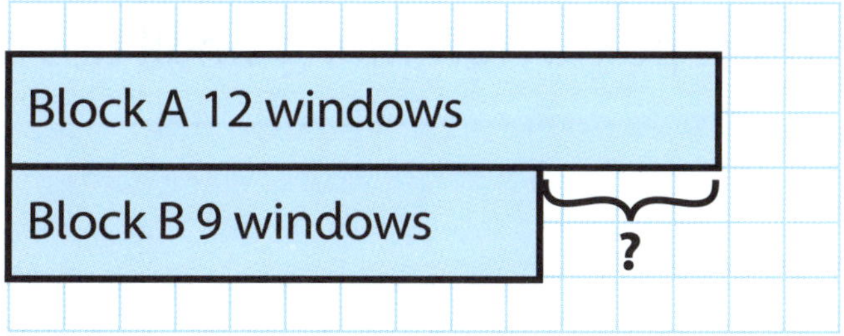

c
- Block B 12 windows
- $\frac{1}{2}$ of B
- ?

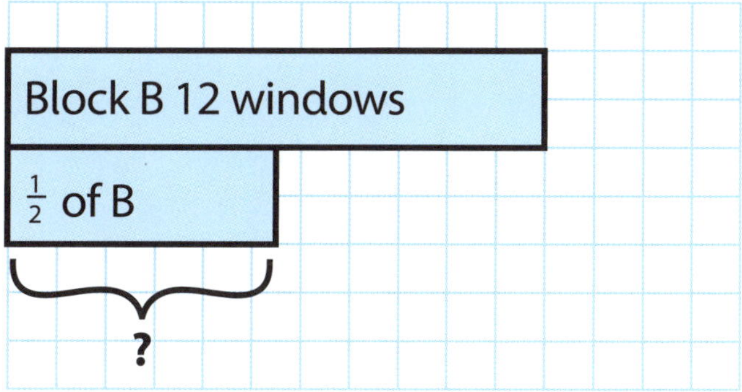

Let's reason ...

The people in an apartment block have a community garden. There is a storage shed in the garden.

The community want to paint the shed orange.
They have no orange paint, but they do have red and yellow paint.

Ani finds this diagram on the internet. It shows how to mix orange paint.

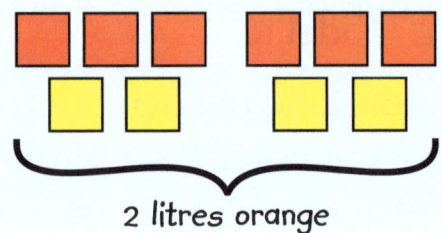

small tins red paint

small tins yellow paint

1 litre orange

2 litres orange

1) To make 2 litres of orange paint:

   a how many small tins of red paint do you need?

   b how many small tins of yellow paint do you need?

2) The community need 5 litres of orange paint. How many small tins of red and yellow paint do they need?

   a Draw or model this problem.

   b Complete the sentence.

   To make 5 litres of orange paint,

   you need ☐ small tins of red paint and ☐ small tins of yellow paint.

Mixing paint

The community want to paint the shed door green. Mandla finds this diagram. It shows how to mix green paint.

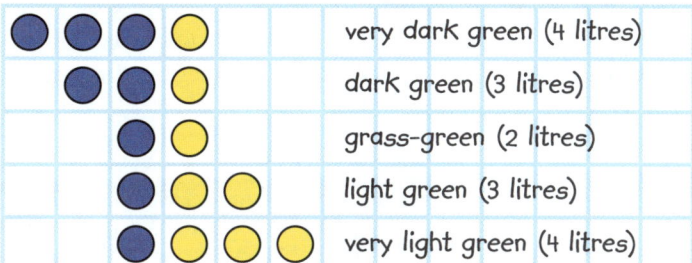

3 How much paint does one circle represent?

_____

4 Draw a model to show what Mandla needs to make:

a 10 litres of grass-green paint

 b 20 litres of very dark green paint.

5 Mandla mixes $\frac{1}{2}$ litre of yellow paint and 1 litre of blue paint.

a What colour does he make?

_____

b Show your partner how you worked this out.

Let's solve …

1. 19 children are playing soccer in the park. 4 children go home. Another 9 children arrive to join the game. How many children are playing soccer now?

   a Draw jumps on the number line to show this problem.

   19

   b Draw dots to model this problem.

   c Show one other way to model this problem.

2. 17 children are playing soccer. 3 children go home and some more children arrive. Now there are two teams with 11 children in each team. How many children arrived? Show your working.

Playing around

Let's reason ...

This indoor play centre has foam blocks that children can play on and build with.

3 Sasha and Jay built these towers with foam blocks.

Sasha's tower

Jay's tower

a Work out how many blocks each child used.

Sasha used _____ blocks.   Jay used _____ blocks.

b Tell your partner how you worked this out.
How did you count blocks that you cannot see?

4 Work with a partner. How many different structures can you build using 4 cubes?

Build models to show the different structures.

Look carefully at your structures. Are any of them really the same, just in different positions?

13

Let's solve ...

1 Read the clues. Where does each person live? Write the first letter of each person's name on their window.

Ani lives on the top floor in the middle apartment.

Nia's window is two floors below Ani's.

Haris lives to the right of Ani but one floor down.

Kai lives on the first floor in the left-hand apartment.

Jo lives on the first floor, but not next to Kai.

Li's window is three floors above Kai's window.

Walid lives on the top floor too.

Pedro's window is above the front door.

2 Daisy Court has 8 floors. There are 40 apartments in the block. Each floor has the same number of apartments.

a How many apartments are there on each floor?
Show how you work this out.

b There are 3 **fire exits** on each floor.
How many fire exits are there altogether?

Who lives there?

3 The lift at Daisy Court takes 42 seconds to get to the 6th floor. It takes 56 seconds to get to the 8th floor. How much longer does it take to get to the 8th floor?

  a Draw a bar model and write a number sentence to show this problem.

  b Solve the problem.

4 An apartment block has 5 floors. There are 21 apartments in the block.

  a How do you know that every floor does not have the same number of apartments? Tell your partner.

  b Read the information. How many apartments are there on each floor? Draw the apartments on the apartment block.

  Each floor has fewer apartments than the floor below it.

  The lowest floor has the most apartments.

  The second floor has 5 apartments.

  The top floor must have at least 2 apartments.

Let's reason ...

1 Aldo makes vegetable soup for his neighbours. He has carrots, potatoes, onions and tomatoes. He always uses 15 vegetables in a pot of soup. He always uses at least one of each type.

  a Show one way Aldo can do this. Write the number of each type of vegetable.

🥕	🥔	🧅	🍅	
				= 15

  b For Monday's soup Aldo uses more onions than carrots or potatoes. Complete the table.

🥕	🥔	🧅	🍅	
				= 15

  c For Wednesday's soup Aldo uses more potatoes than any other type of vegetable. Complete the table.

🥕	🥔	🧅	🍅	
				= 15

2 Aldo gives two bowls of soup to each of his neighbours. He gives away 12 bowls altogether.

  a How many neighbours does he have? _____

  b How did you work this out? Tick ✓ a box.

| I modelled the problem with objects. ☐ | I did a drawing. ☐ | I subtracted twos. ☐ | I did something else. ☐ |

Sharing with our neighbours

Let's solve ...

3 Didem makes two trays of baklava for her 8 neighbours. She gives an **equal** share to each neighbour. Draw lines on the trays to show how she can do this.

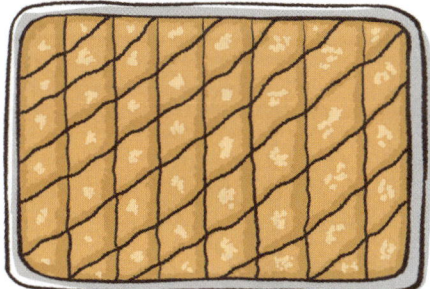 

4 There are 14 samosas on the table. Four friends eat an equal number of the samosas.

a What is the greatest number of samosas that each person can eat?

b Everyone wants to eat the same number of samosas with none **left over**. How many more samosas do the friends need?

5 Lee buys a box of 30 figs. She gives the same number of figs to each of her 3 neighbours. She has 12 figs left over. How many figs does she give to each neighbour?

➡ Turn back to page 4 and complete the problem-solving record.

2 Trees and forests

Think, talk, write

Look at the page from Mai's sticker book.

Measuring trees

1. Answer these questions with a partner.

   a. How can you use the grid to compare the heights of the trees? Tell your partner.

   b. Which tree is the tallest? Tree _____

   c. Which trees are the same height?

   Tree _____ and Tree _____   Tree _____ and Tree _____

2. The sticker for Tree H is missing. Tree H is taller than Tree B but shorter than Tree C. Draw Tree H on the grid.

3. The branch of a small tree is 40 cm long. It grows 5 cm each year.

   a. How long is the branch after 1 year?

   _____

   b. How many years does it take for the branch to be 70 cm long?

   _____

4. The tallest tree in a school garden is 12 metres tall. The shortest tree is 7 metres shorter than the tallest tree.

   a. Draw a bar model to show this.

   b. Work out the height of the shortest tree in the garden.

   _____

19

Let's reason ...

The tallest type of tree in the world is the Hyperion. Hyperion trees can grow to 116 metres.

1. Read these clues. Work out the heights of the other tall trees. Write the height of each tree.

   The Raven's Tower is 3 m shorter than 100 m.

   The Giant Sequoia is 2 m shorter than the Raven's Tower.

   The Raven's Tower is 5 m taller than the White Knight.

   The Alpine Ash is between 80 and 90 m tall. Both the digits are the same.

   The Giant Sequoia is 10 m taller than the King Stringy.

2. The three tallest types of trees are in California, USA. The others are in Tasmania, Australia.

   a Circle the trees that are in California.

   b What is the tallest type of tree in Tasmania?

3. A giraffe is 5 m tall. How many giraffes tall is a Giant Sequoia?

The tallest trees in the world

Think, talk, draw

4 a What can you see on the chart? Tell your partner.

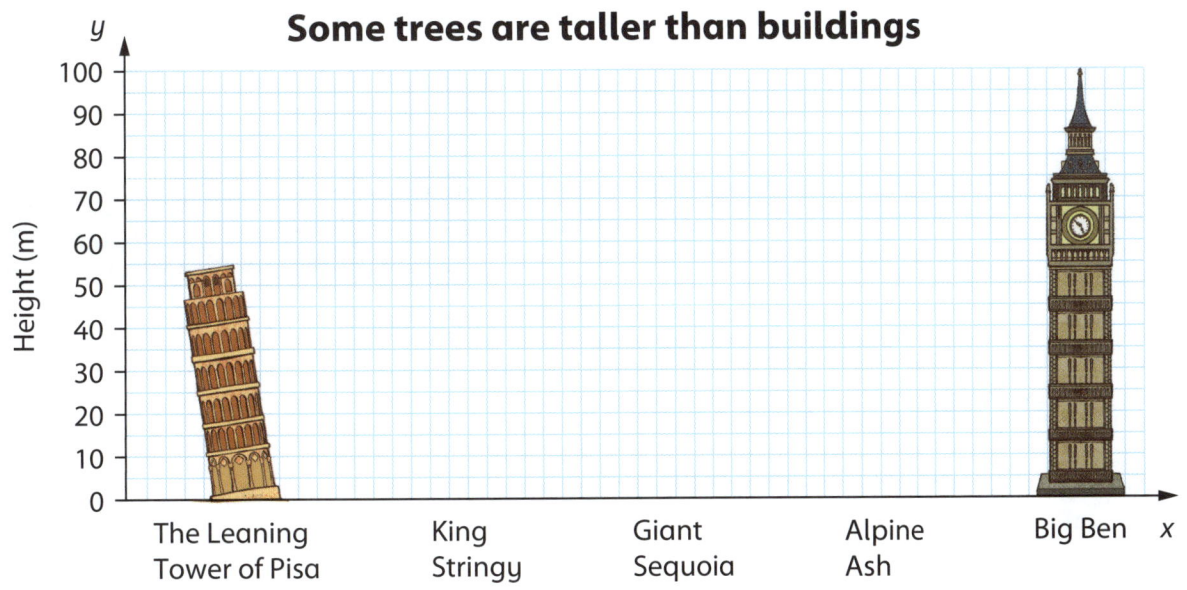

b Show the heights of a King Stringy, a Giant Sequoia and an Alpine Ash on the chart.

5 Jabu wrote a word problem using the information on his chart. Look at the way he worked out the solution.

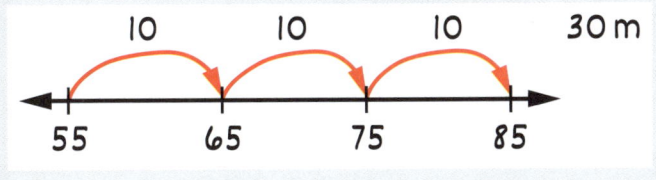

What is the difference between the heights of the Leaning Tower of Pisa and a King Stringy?

a Write a word problem using the chart. Show how to solve it.

My problem _____   My solution

b Swap with your partner. Check each other's solutions.

21

Trees grow a new layer of wood **around** their trunk every year.

When a tree is cut down, you can see rings on the tree stump. Each ring is the growth from one year.

To find out the age of the tree, count the dark rings. Start at the centre.

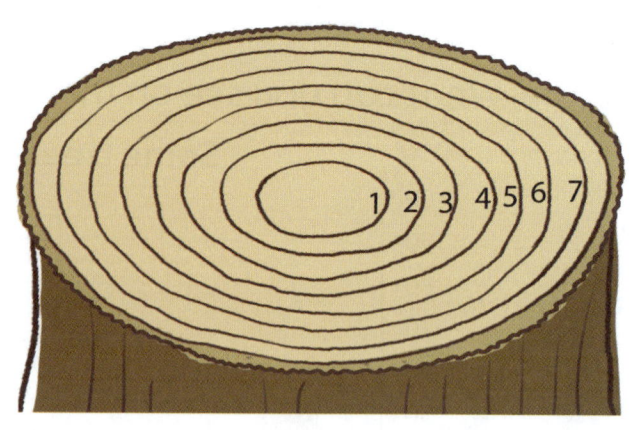

This tree was 7 years old when it was cut down.

1 Look at these tree stumps. Write the age of each tree when it was cut down.

Draw a tree stump to match the information.

a _____ years old — a tree 2 years older

b _____ years old — a tree 1 year younger

c _____ years old — a tree half this age

d _____ years old — a tree planted 3 years before this one

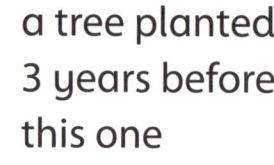

22

How old is that tree?

2 These three trees were all cut down at the same time.

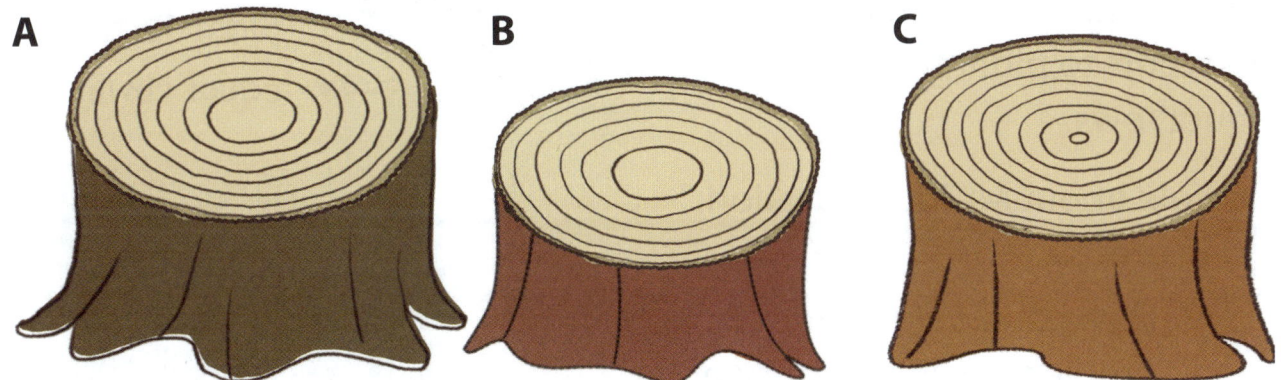

a Which tree was planted first? _____

How do you know? _____

b Which tree was the youngest? _____

c Naresh is 12. How old was he when Tree B was first planted? _____

3 This tree was cut down today.

a How many years ago was it first planted? _____

b Can the snake wrap itself around the tree stump so that its nose touches the end of its tail? Work with a partner to decide.

Let's reason ...

① Mr Tau has 12 trees to plant. He wants to plant the trees in equal rows.

I wonder how many different ways I can plant 12 trees in equal rows.

a Talk about Mr Tau's question in groups.
  • How can you act out this problem to find an answer?
  • What can you use to model this problem?
  • Think of some other ways to solve the problem.

b Choose one of the methods.
  Then solve the problem and answer Mr Tau's question.

  There are ☐ ways to plant 12 trees in equal rows.

② Draw all the ways you can find to plant these groups of trees in equal rows.

  a 16 trees

  b 20 trees

24

Planting trees

Let's solve …

3 A school has some trees to plant on Arbor Day.

The block diagram shows how many of each type of tree they have.

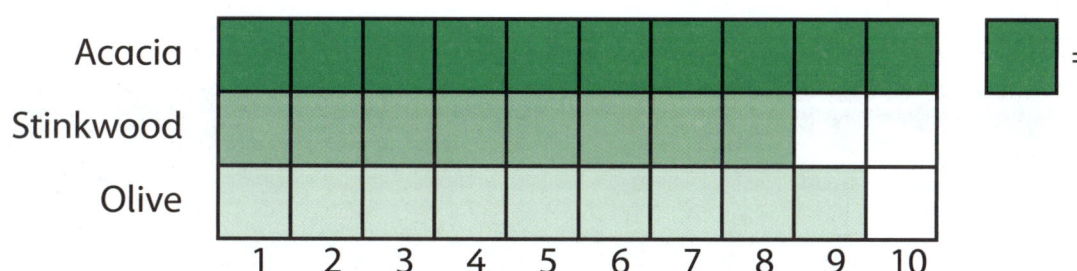

a How many trees does the school have altogether? Show how you work this out.

_____

b Read the information and work out how many trees each class will plant.

Class 1 will plant half of the acacia trees and 3 olive trees.

Class 2 will plant one-quarter of the stinkwood trees and half of the remaining olive trees.

Class 3 will plant the rest of the trees.

Class 1 _____ trees   Class 2 _____ trees   Class 3 _____ trees

4 A community wants to plant 100 trees. They plant 19 trees in March. Then each month they plant 5 more trees than in the previous month.

In which month will they plant the 100th tree?

_____

Show how you worked this out.

25

Think, talk, solve

1. Work in groups.

   - What can you learn about rainforests from this picture?
   - What questions can you ask about the rainforest in the picture?

2. An animal walks past three trees on its way to the water. Use the clues to match each tree to its name.

   The animal walks past the rubber tree before it walks past the Brazil nut tree.

   The kapok tree is not the first tree it walks past.

   The Brazil nut is not the last tree it walks past.

kapok tree   Brazil nut tree   rubber tree

In the rainforest

3 Show how you solve each problem.

a A monkey ate 43 berries and 19 insects. How many more berries did it eat than insects?

b A scientist counts 24 parrots in two trees. One tree has 2 more than the other. How many parrots are in each tree?

4 The pictures show the three main causes of rainforest destruction.

agriculture   logging   cattle grazing

a Write 1, 2 and 3 on the pictures to order them from most destructive to least destructive.

b Tell your partner how you decided on the order.

5 A lemur wants to jump from tree 1 to get the ripe fruit in tree 11. It can jump 2, 3 or 4 trees in each jump. Draw a route the lemur can take to get to the fruit.

Let's solve ...

A community has a piece of land that is divided into blocks.
The plan of their land is on page 29.

1 Answer these questions.

   a How many blocks of land are shown on the plan? _____

   b How many blocks of land does each of these cover?

      the road _____ the dam _____ the forest _____

   c In which blocks is each of these?

      the bird hide _____ Gate A _____

      Gate B _____

   d Mali is in block D7. Where is she? _____

   e The highest tree in the forest is found in block H4. Draw a dot on the map to show where it is.

2 There are 20 trees in each block of the forest.

- $\frac{1}{2}$ are kapok trees.
- $\frac{1}{4}$ are Brazil nut trees.
- 2 are palm trees.
- The rest are mango trees.

   a How many mango trees are there in a block?

   _____

   b How many palm trees are there in the forest area that is to the left of the road?

   _____

   c How did you work out the number of each type of tree? Tell your partner what you did.

Map it out

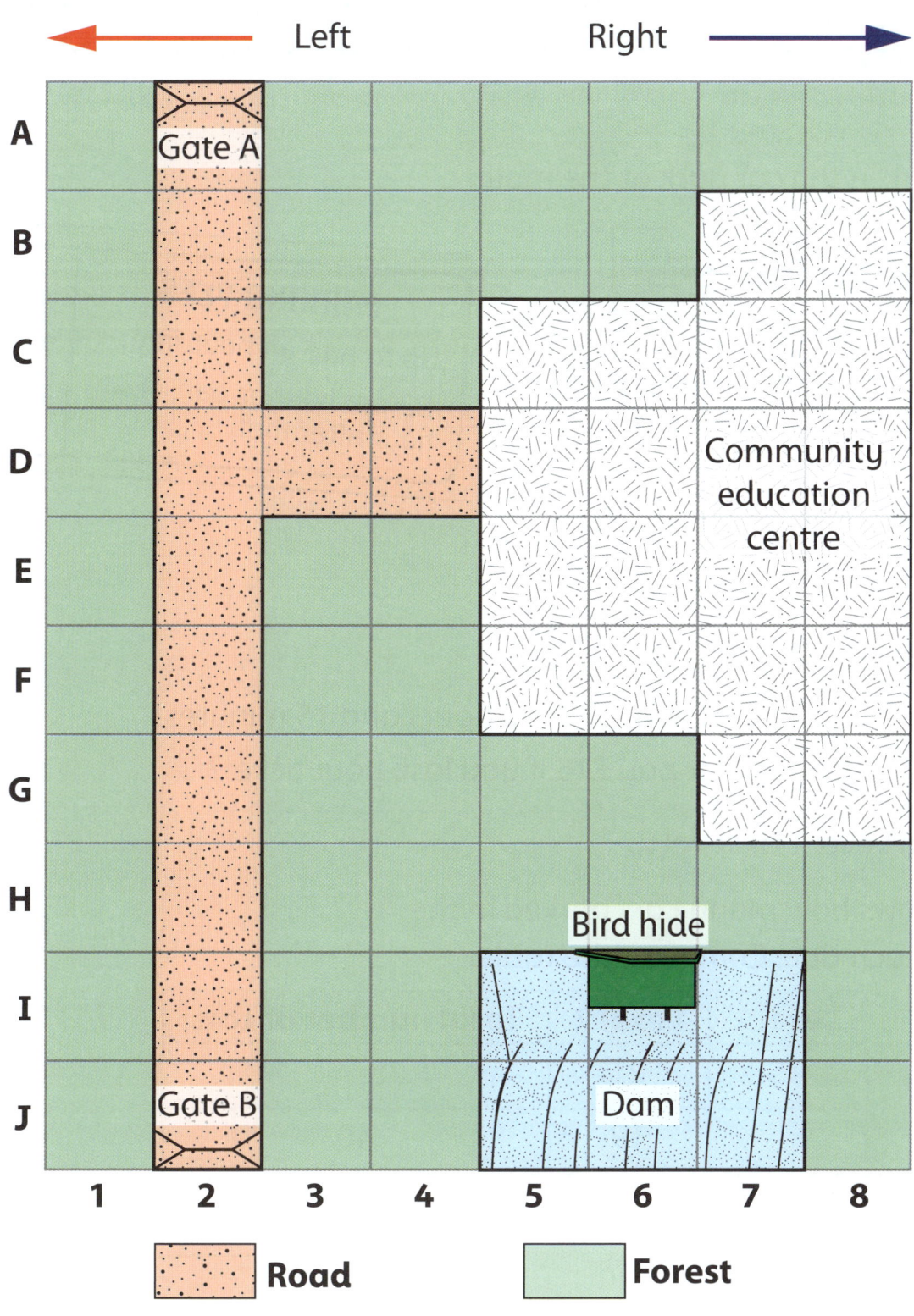

→ Turn back to page 4 and complete the problem-solving record.

3 Let's go shopping

Think, talk, write

Mai and her dad park in the car park at the mall.

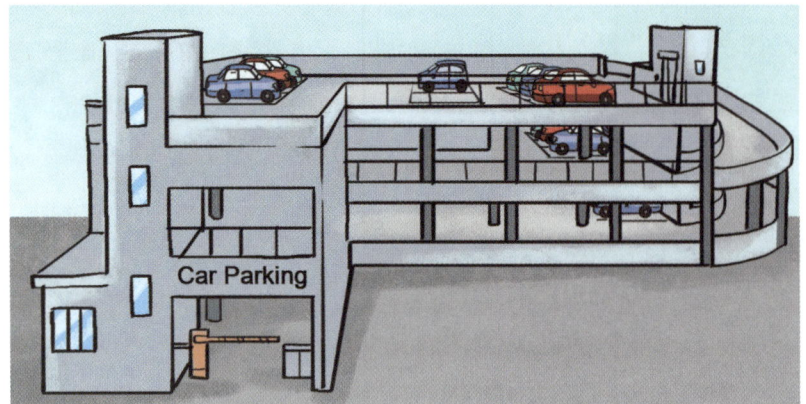

PARKING FEES
Up to half an hour free.
£2 per hour or part of an hour after that.

Fine for lost ticket £15

1 Talk about these questions with a partner.

  a How much do you pay to park for:
   • 15 minutes?   • 2 hours?   • 2 hours and 15 minutes?

  b Why do you think you must pay £15 if you lose your ticket?

2 Cars can park on Level 1 or Level 2.

  a The table shows how many cars parked in the car park on each day. Complete the table.

	Level 1	Level 2	Total number of cars
Monday	15	21	
Tuesday		19	40
Wednesday	25		35

  b On Thursday, there are 24 cars on Level 2. Half of the cars are white, one-quarter of the cars are silver. Three cars are black. The rest are blue. How many blue cars are there?

   ☐ blue cars

At the shops

3 Draw lines to match each car to the correct parking fee.

2 hours   3½ hours   45 minutes   25 minutes

£0   £2   £8   £4

4 How much **change** will each person get if they pay for parking with a £20 note?

Parking fee	£10	£6	£12	£15 fine
Change				

5 Mai and her dad go to the fish counter. Customers take a ticket to be served.

a Their number is 39. How many customers will be served before them?

b They see their neighbour, Mrs Khan, at the fish counter. She has ticket number 47. How many people will be served before Mrs Khan?

Let's reason ...

1. Jamiah has a flower stall. She makes different-sized bunches of flowers. Each bunch has at least 6 flowers and not more than 10 flowers.

   Write all the possible numbers of flowers in a bunch.

2. **a** Jamiah fills this box with flowers. Read the clues. Draw flowers in the box to match the clues. You must fill the whole box.

   There are only 4 colours.

   At least 6 are red.

   No more than 3 are pink.

   At least 2 are yellow.

   Exactly $\frac{1}{2}$ are orange.

   b Can you find any different answers to the same problem? Share your ideas in your group.

At the flower stall

Let's solve ...

Here are some bunches of flowers on Jamiah's stall.

3) Solve the problems. Draw or write to show how you worked it out.

a) Bennu wants to buy 2 yellow bunches and 1 red bunch. How much money does she need?

b) Mees has £9. He buys 1 purple bunch. He has enough money left to buy 1 more bunch. Which bunch can he buy?

c) Mona has £12. She buys 2 purple bunches. What can she buy with the change?

d) Tarek buys 1 red bunch, 1 yellow bunch and 1 orange bunch. He pays with a £20 note. How much change does he get?

33

Think, talk, solve

Discuss each problem with your group before you work it out. Show your working.

1 Mr Gallo opens his ice cream shop at 10 o'clock in the morning. He closes the shop at 6 o'clock in the evening. How many hours is the shop open?

_____

2 It takes 4 hours for the ice cream to freeze.

a Mr Gallo puts some chocolate ice cream into the freezer at 10 o'clock. At what time will the ice cream be frozen?

b The vanilla ice cream must be frozen by half past 4. At what time must Mr Gallo put it into the freezer?

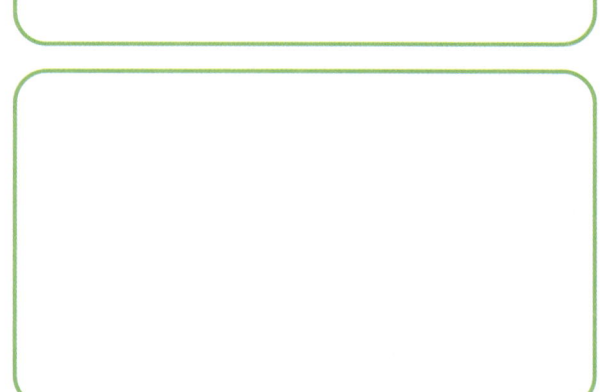

3 Li buys 6 cones. Each cone has 3 scoops of ice cream. How many scoops of ice cream are there altogether?

The ice cream shop

4 The ice cream shop sells special 2-scoop cones. There are 4 flavours to choose from: vanilla, chocolate, strawberry and mango.

  a How many different 2-scoop cones can you make?
  Each cone must have 2 different flavours.
  Show your working in the box.

  I think you can make ☐ different cones.

  b Talk about your answer with a partner.
  Have you found all the different cones?
  How do you know if you have found them all?

  c One special 2-scoop cone costs £5. What is the cost for 2 cones?

5 What is the missing amount? Tell your partner how you worked it out.

 +  +  = £18

 +  = £8

 +  =

Think, talk, draw

1 There are 48 cherries in a box.

a How can you arrange the cherries to make them easier to count?

> Can you use cubes or counters to help you work this out?

Draw two different ways.

b The shopkeeper sells half the cherries in a full box to Ms Lee. He sells half of the rest of the cherries to Mr Lim. The shopkeeper eats half of the remaining cherries at lunchtime.

How many cherries are left in the box?

How can you colour this grid to help you solve the problem?

☐ cherries are left in the box.

Packaging problems

Let's reason…

2 Mrs Klein owns a bakery. She displays the baked goods on two shelves.

a Mrs Klein has made 6 fruit tarts.

How many different ways can she put the tarts on the shelves?

Use the table to record all the ways you can find.

Top shelf								
Bottom shelf								

b How can you be sure you have found all the ways? Tell your group.

3 Kari wants to buy fruit for a class picnic. The fruit is sold in these bags. The number of each fruit is shown on the bag.

Kari wants to buy at least 50 fruits, but no more than 55. He wants to have a mix of different fruits.

a Show two different ways that Kari can do this.

b Compare your answers in your group. How many different ways did your group find? Tell each other how you worked out your answers.

Think, talk, write

1 A clothes shop is having a **half-price sale**.

What does that mean? Share your ideas with your group.

2 Look at how some students worked out half of 12.

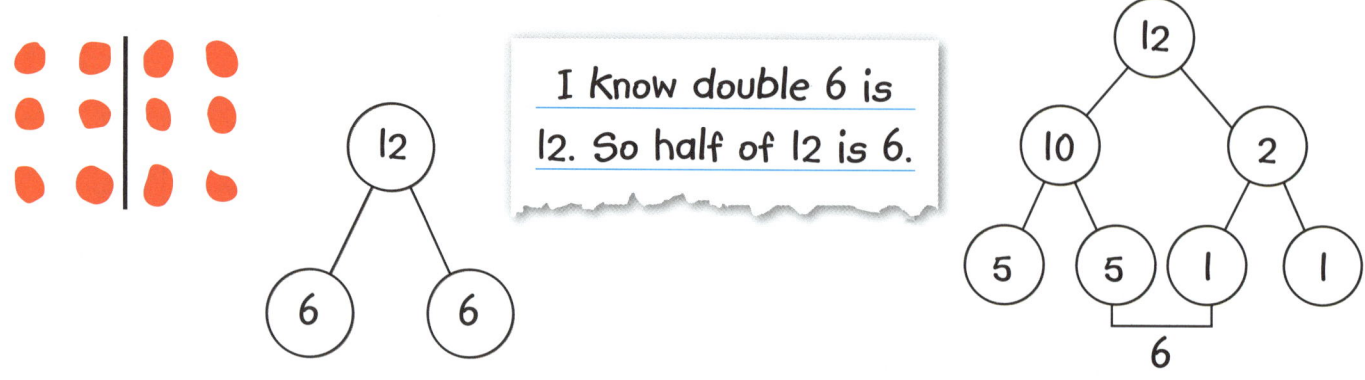

Talk about these questions with a partner.
- What did each student do?
- How do you find half of 12? Why?

3 What is the sale price of each item?

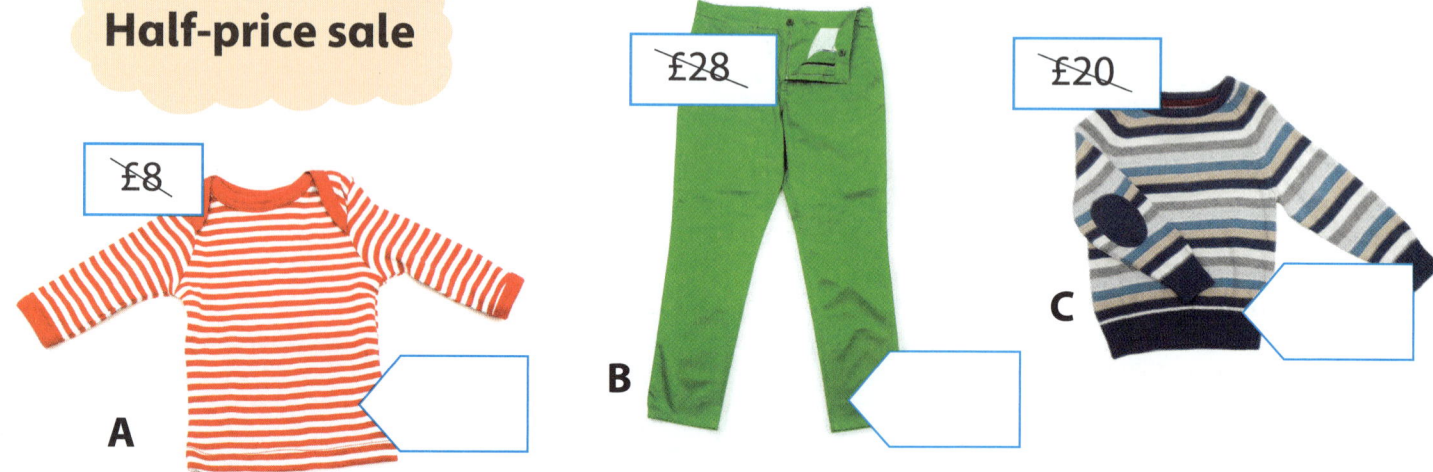

It's on sale

Let's solve ...

④ A shop offers £5 off the price of each jacket.

   a What was the price of each jacket before the £5 was taken off?

   b How did you work out the answers? You can tick ✓ more than one box.

| I counted on my fingers. ☐ | I did jumps on a number line. ☐ | I skip counted. ☐ | I added. ☐ | I did something else. ☐ |

Think, talk, write

1. These bracelets are on sale at a school fete.

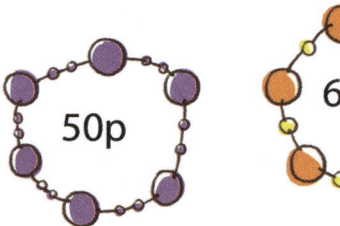 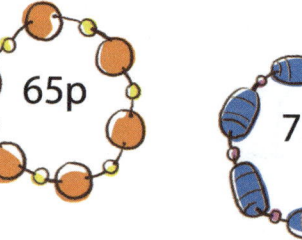 

50p 65p 75p 84p

Remember, there are 100 pence in 1 pound.

£1 = 100p

£1.20 = £1 + 20p

= 100p + 20p

= 120p

What strategies can you use to solve these problems? Discuss your ideas with a partner.

a) What is the change from £1 for each bracelet?

b) A customer buys all 4 bracelets and pays with £5. What is the customer's change? Think of two different strategies.

2. Work with a partner. Complete the table.

Price	Money paid	Change	Is the change correct?	Draw the correct change.
£1.45	two £1 coins	two 20p coins and one 5p coin	Yes / No	
£9.75	two £5 notes	two 5p coins, one 50p coin, two 5p coins	Yes / No	
£8.80	£10 note	two £1 coins and one 20p coin	Yes / No	

Check your change

Let's solve ...

3 Jan and Luigi each bought 1 item at the store.
They each paid with a £5 note. Here is their change.

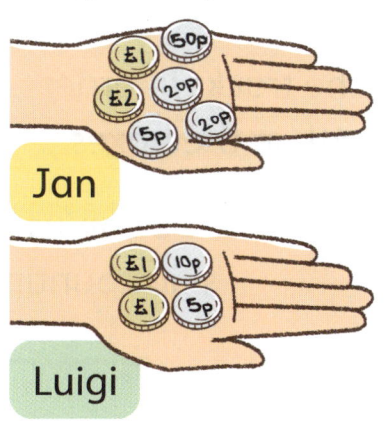

a How do you know they did not buy the same item? Tell your partner.

b What item did Jan buy? _____

c What item did Luigi buy? _____

4 Molly bought two marker pens at the art shop.
She paid with a £20 note and got £12 change.

£20		
£12	?	?

a Work out the price of each marker pen.

How can the bar model help you solve the problem?

_____

b How many marker pens can Molly buy for £15?

_____

5 Lisa bought a pack of marker pens for £8.25. She paid with a £10 note.

What coins did Lisa get in her change? Use the smallest number of coins possible.

_____

➡ Turn back to page 4 and complete the problem-solving record.

41

4 Sports day

Let's reason …

1. Look at the cone tracks.

   a First, guess which track has the highest total. Put the tracks in order from highest to lowest total. Write 1st, 2nd, 3rd or 4th in the boxes. 1st is for the highest total and 4th is for the lowest.

   b Add up all the numbers in each track and write the totals in the circles.

   > You can use skip counting.

   My guesses:

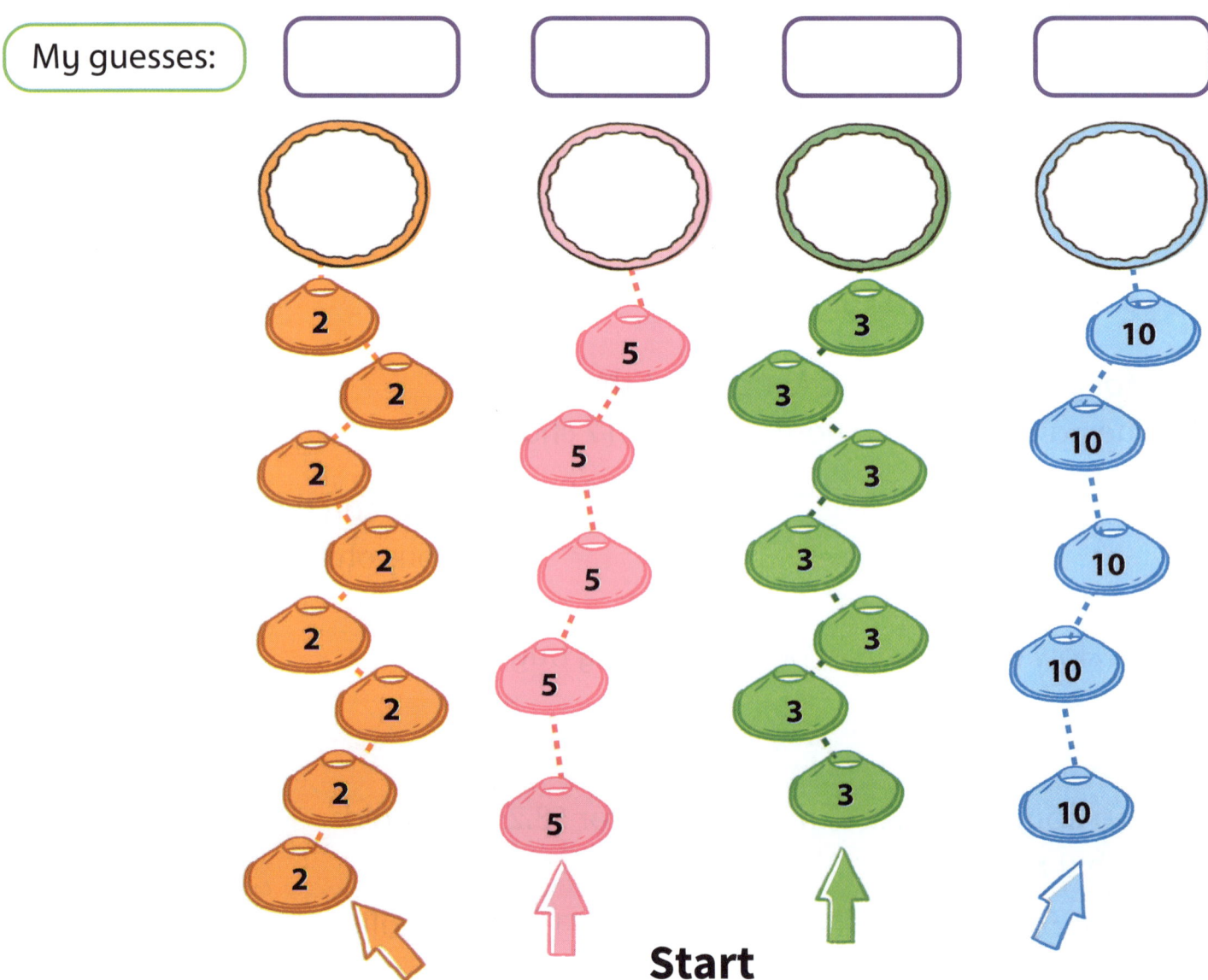

2. Tell a partner how you guessed. Talk about whether you were right.

Counting cones

3 a You cannot use skip counting to find the totals for these cone tracks. Explain why to a partner.

b The totals are all mixed up. Work out which total belongs to each track. Draw a line to match each total to the correct track.

> Look at the numbers in each track. Which numbers can you group to make easier sums?

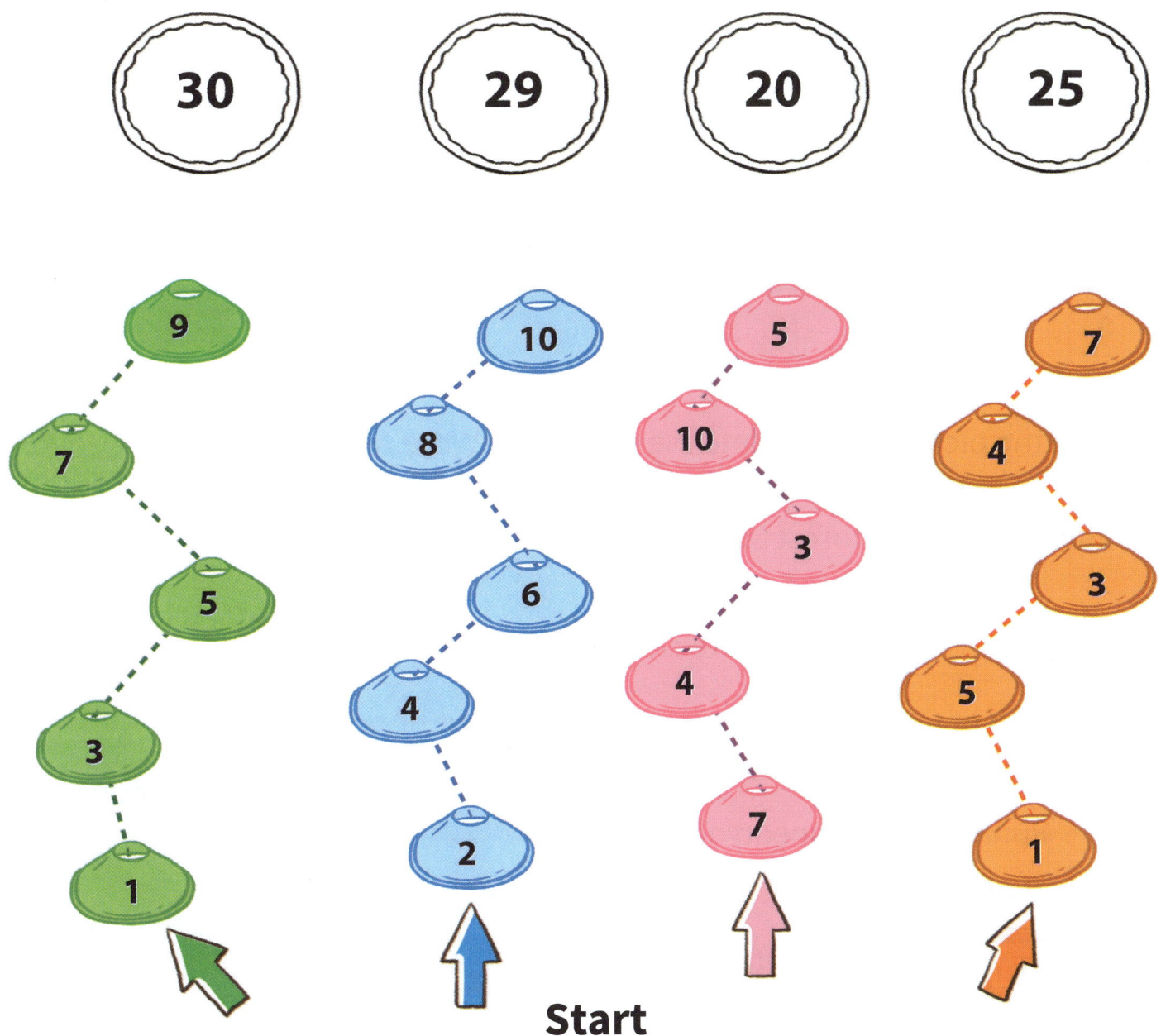

c Work with a partner to check your answers.

Think, talk, solve

Five runners are taking part in the 100-metre race. This is a **birds-eye-view** of the race. It shows the runners from above.

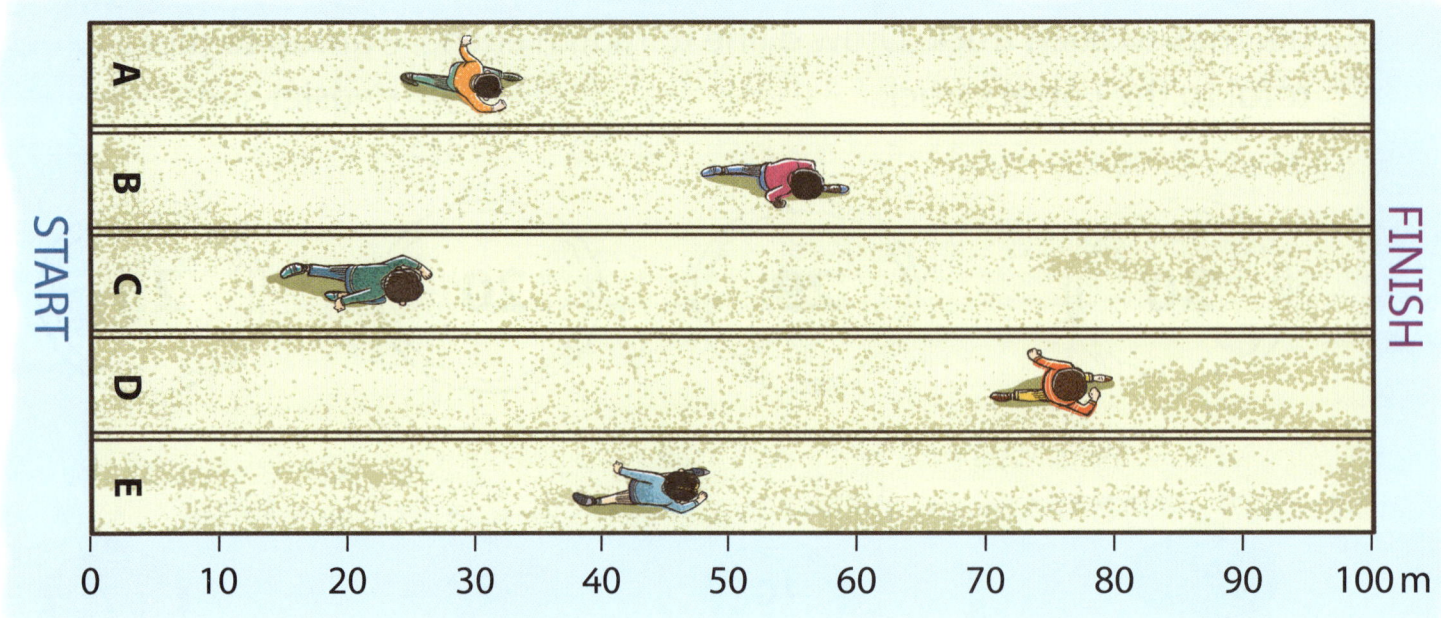

1 Use the picture to complete the sentences. Write A, B, C, D or E.

Runner ☐ is closest to the finish line.   Runner ☐ is in second place.

Runners ☐ and ☐ are closest to the halfway mark.

2 The end of the race was a surprise. Read what happened. Work out who came first, second and third.

- Runner A went ahead of Runner B.
- Then Runner E went ahead of Runner A.

> Ahead means in front of.

> You can draw on the track to show the new positions.

Runner ☐   Runner ☐   Runner ☐

44

The 100 m race

3 Another 100 m race is taking place on the running track.

Read the clues and draw each runner's position. Draw a simple shape for each runner.

Runner A is halfway between the start and the finish.

Runner B is 30 m ahead of Runner A.

Runner C is 10 m behind the finish.

Runner E is 20 m behind Runner D.

Runner D is 20 m behind Runner A.

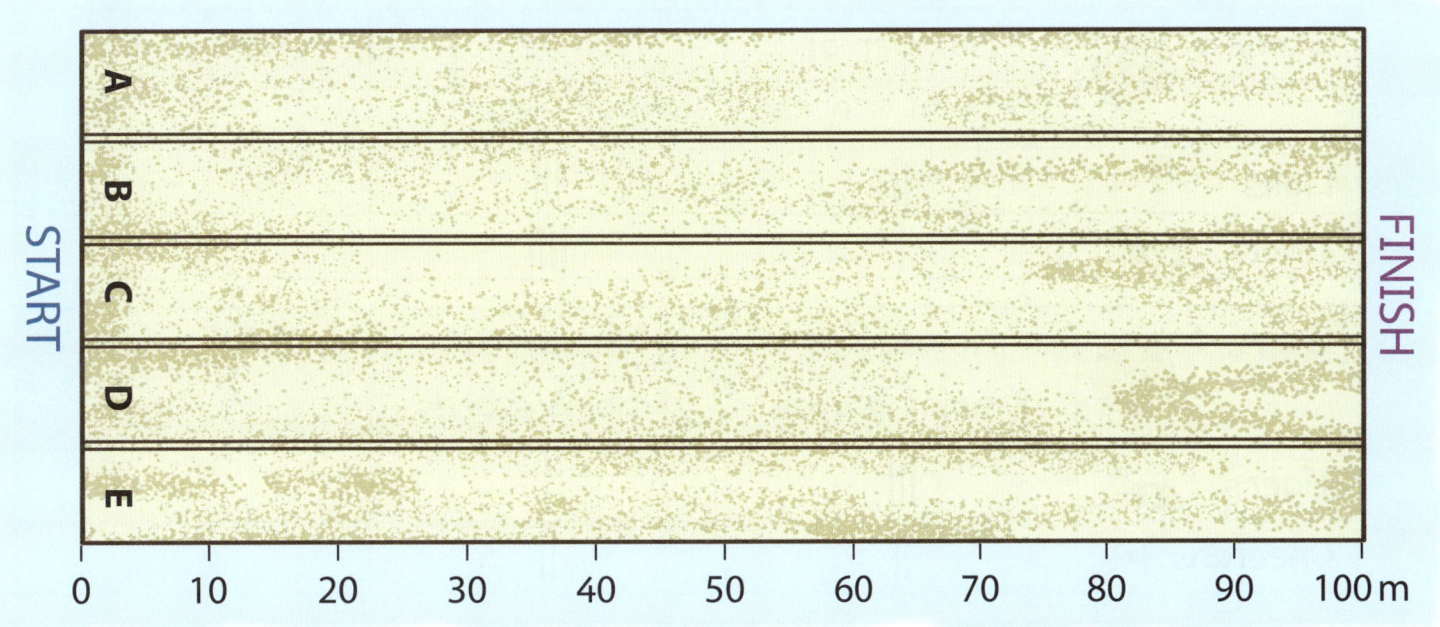

4 How many metres is each runner from the finish line?

Runner A _____   Runner B _____

Runner C _____   Runner D _____

Runner E _____

Let's solve …

In basketball, you get points for getting the ball **through** the hoop.

- If you score from outside the 3-point line, you get 3 points.
- If you score from inside the 3-point line, you get 2 points.

1 There were 3 basketball games at sports day.

These **tally tables** show how many times each team scored.

Game 1	Number of 3-point scores	Number of 2-point scores	Total points
Lions	||	|||	
Tigers	|	||||	

Game 2	Number of 3-point scores	Number of 2-point scores	Total points
Tigers	|||	|	
Cheetahs	||	||	

Game 3	Number of 3-point scores	Number of 2-point scores	Total points
Cheetahs	|||	||	
Lions	|||	||||	

a Work out the total points for each team in each game. Complete the tables.

b Each team played in 2 games. Work out how many points each team scored altogether.

Lions: _____   Tigers: _____   Cheetahs: _____

Basketball hoops

2 Some students played a game to practise shooting hoops. They each had 12 throws.

> Shoot hoops means throw balls at the basketball hoop. A score is a throw that goes into the hoop. A miss is a throw that does not go into the hoop.

Half of Mike's throws went into the hoop.

Sani scored on one-third of his throws.

Mahle missed one-quarter of her throws.

Write each student's total number of scores.

Mike _____   Sani _____   Mahle _____

3 Lizzie, Dennis and Veena also practised shooting hoops. Read the clues. Work out the number of scores and misses for each person.

Each student had an equal number of throws.

The total number of scores was 17.

Lizzie scored on half of her throws.

Dennis missed one-quarter of his throws.

The total number of throws (scores and misses altogether) was 24.

	Scores	Misses
Lizzie		
Dennis		
Veena		

Let's reason ...

To **eliminate** means to remove or throw away. Clues help us to eliminate wrong answers, so we can **deduce** the correct answer. To deduce means to work out the answer using facts we already know.

1 The clues tell you how many eggs to put in the box.

   a Read each clue and cross out the numbers that the clue eliminates.

   b Deduce the correct number of eggs. Draw the eggs in the box.

   Clues:

   The number of eggs is not even.

   The number of eggs is greater than 2 and less than 10.

   The number of eggs is 2 less than the greatest remaining number in the list.

   Possible number of eggs in the box:

1	2	3	4	5	6	7	8	9	10	11	12

The egg-and-spoon race

Let's solve ...

> Remember, there are 60 seconds in 1 minute.

2 Three students ran in the egg-and-spoon race. Read the clues. Deduce each student's finishing time and their team.

The student from Team A finished 5 seconds after the student from Team B.

Erin finished in exactly 1 and a half minutes.

Lily finished before Jack.

		Time in seconds			Team		
		65	85	90	A	B	C
Name	Erin						
	Lily						
	Jack						
Team	A						
	B						
	C						

Think, talk, write

In the obstacle race, you must get **over**, around, through or **under** each obstacle.

1 a How will you pass each obstacle? Circle the word that describes what you will do.

b Think of another way to pass each obstacle. Underline the word.

c Describe to a partner your two different ways to pass each obstacle.

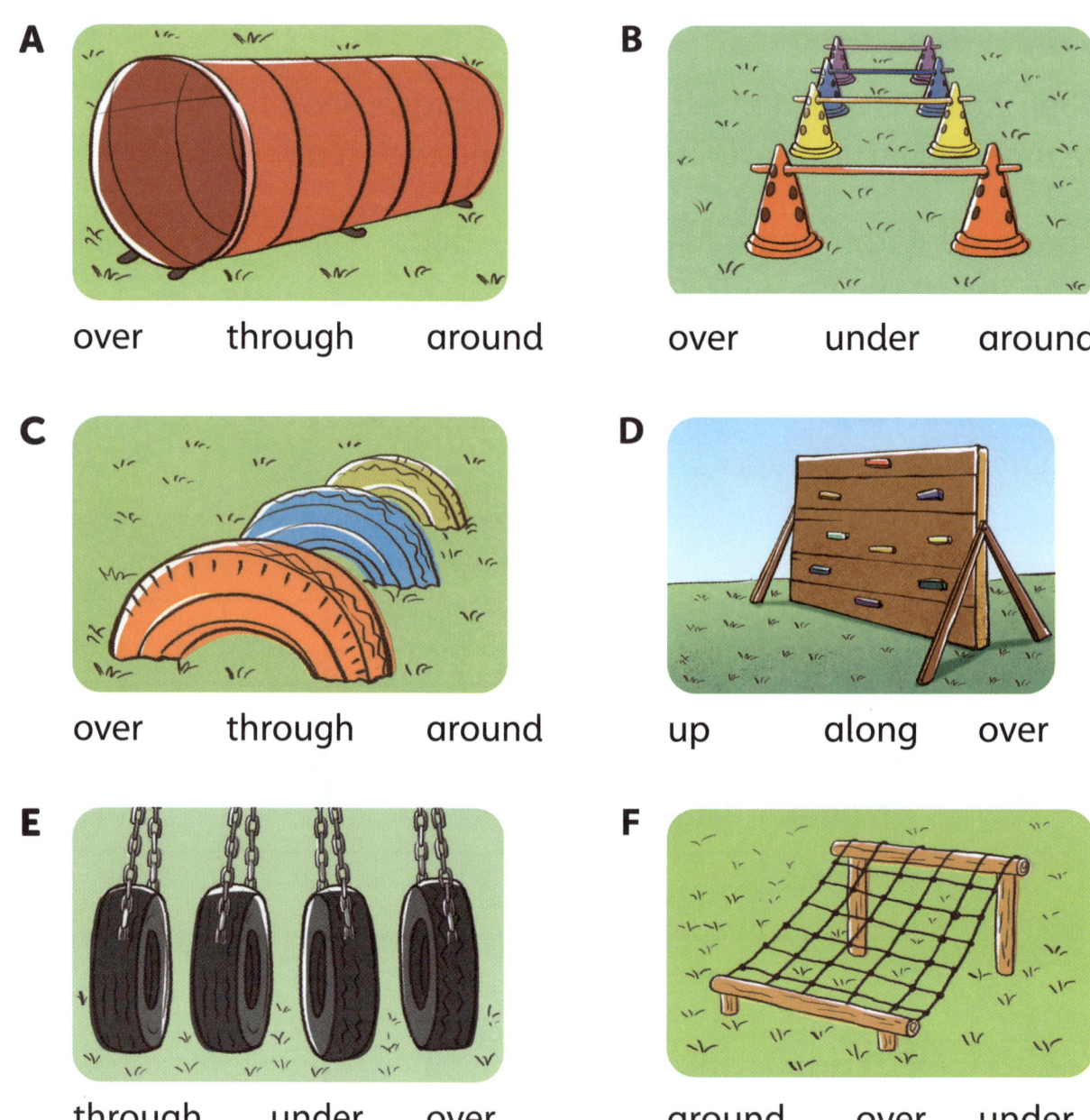

A   over   through   around

B   over   under   around

C   over   through   around

D   up   along   over

E   through   under   over

F   around   over   under

The obstacle race

Let's solve …

② Design your own obstacle for an obstacle race.
Use at least one option from each box.

2D shapes
circle
square
triangle
rectangle

3D shapes
ball
cube
cuboid
cylinder

Ways to pass the obstacle
over
through
up
along

Think, talk, solve

1 The table shows Suna and Ali's times for each obstacle in the obstacle course. Use the times to answer the questions on page 53.

Obstacle	Suna	Ali
A tube	25 seconds	20 seconds
B cones	12 seconds	14 seconds
C half-tyres	18 seconds	30 seconds
D wall	5 minutes	3 minutes
E hanging tyres	$6\frac{1}{2}$ minutes	8 minutes
F low net	30 seconds	$\frac{1}{2}$ minute

Keeping time

2 Work with a partner. Complete the sentences. Write the correct letter A, B, C, D, E or F. Discuss how to work it out.

a Ali and Suna had equal times on obstacle _____.

b Suna was 2 seconds faster than Ali on obstacle _____.

c Ali was 2 minutes faster than Suna on obstacle _____.

d Suna was 5 seconds slower than Ali on obstacle _____.

3 Work in a team. Make your own challenge with two different activities. The pictures show some ideas.

a How long can each student in the team do each activity? Record the times in the table.

Name	Activity 1 _____	Activity 2 _____

hula hoop

balancing on one foot

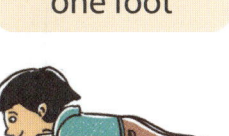

plank

balancing an object

b Use your table to complete the two sentences.

In Activity 1, _____'s time was the longest.

In Activity 2, _____'s time was the shortest.

→ Turn back to page 4 and complete the problem-solving record.

53

5 Growing plants

1. Chiku planted a bean. She drew a picture of the bean plant each week. But she mixed up the pictures.

   a. Talk to a partner. How can you work out the week number of each picture?

   b. Complete the information under each picture.

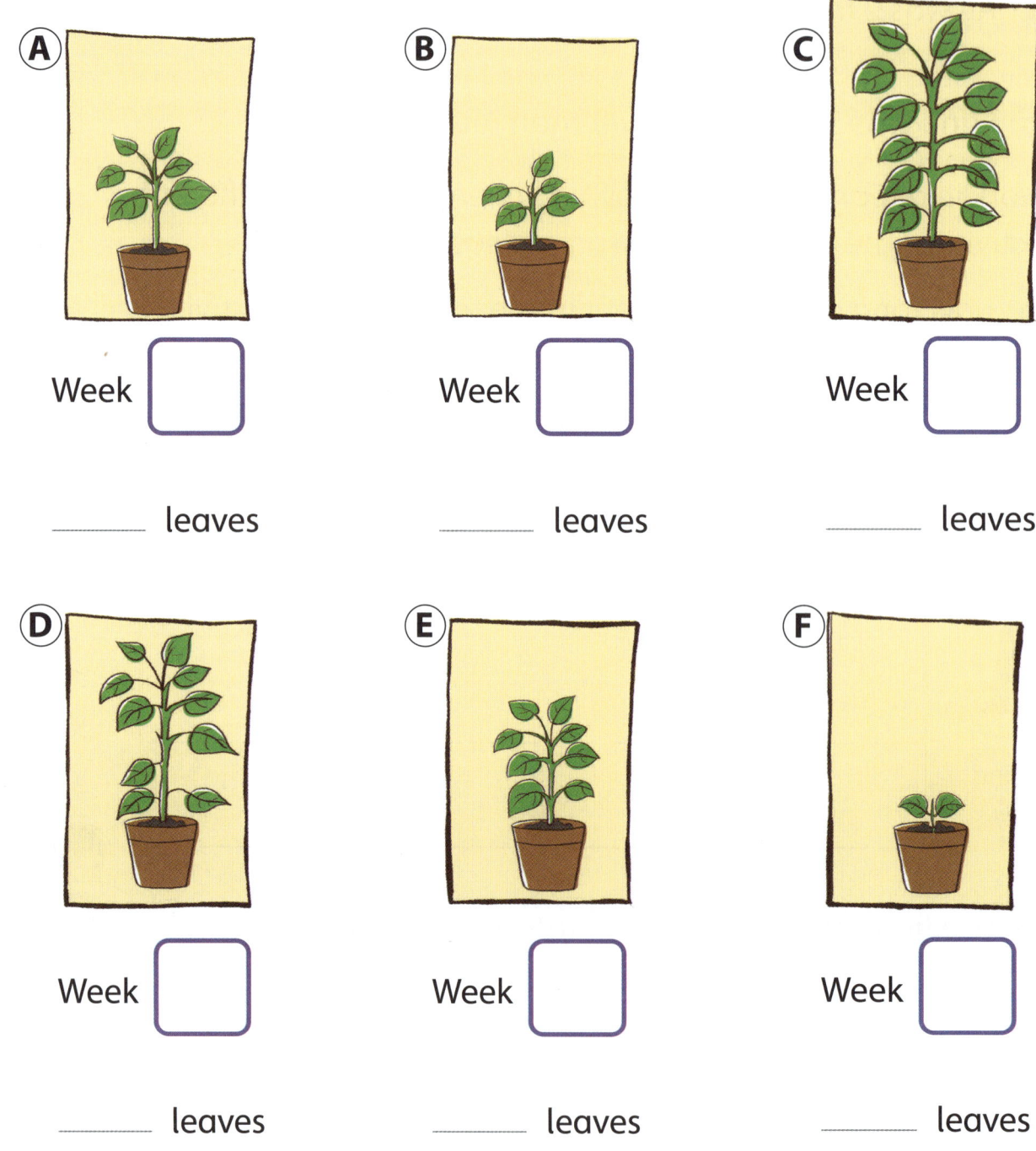

A Week ☐ ____ leaves

B Week ☐ ____ leaves

C Week ☐ ____ leaves

D Week ☐ ____ leaves

E Week ☐ ____ leaves

F Week ☐ ____ leaves

Planting a bean

2 Chiku wants to count the seeds in each packet. She makes shapes and patterns with the seeds to help her count.

a What shape or pattern did Chiku make with each type of seed? Tell a partner.

b Count the seeds from each packet. Write the numbers next to the correct type.

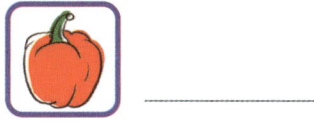  

c Where does each number fit on the number line? Write the letter for each seed packet in the correct position.

Think, talk, write

A seed tray is useful for planting seeds.

1 Luca plants tomato and spinach seeds. He puts one type of seed in each space in the seed tray. The diagram shows how he arranged the seeds.

a True or false:

Number of tomato seeds = Number of spinach seeds

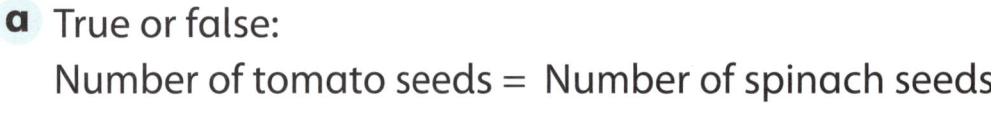

b How did you work it out? Tick ✓ the strategies you used.

I counted the tomatoes and the spinach. ☐	I counted in 2s. ☐	I saw that every row has 2 tomatoes and 2 spinach. ☐	I saw the pattern without counting. ☐	I used my own strategy. ☐

My strategy:

Using seed trays

2 a Luca puts 2 seeds in each space in the seed tray. How many tomato seeds are there altogether? Choose one of these strategies to work it out.

- Number line:

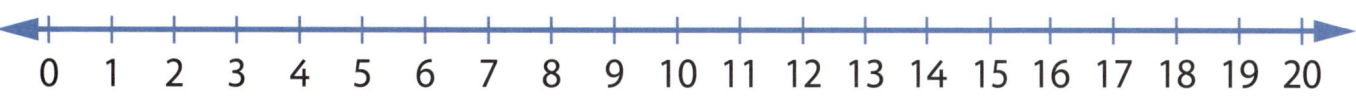

- Multiplying (times): _____

- Adding: _____

- A picture or model:

My answer: He used  seeds.

b Now use one of the other strategies to check your answer.

Let's solve ...

1. Rosa has 12 seeds to plant in the garden. She wants to plant them in rows, with an equal number of seeds in each row. She wants to make more than 1 row and fewer than 8 rows.

   She draws three ways.

   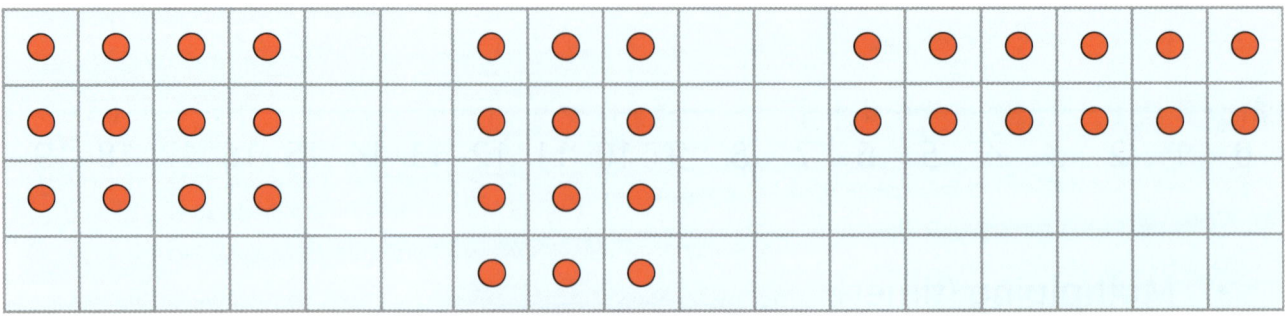

   | 3 rows | 4 rows | 2 rows |
   | 4 seeds per row | 3 seeds per row | 6 seeds per row |

   a. How does the diagram help?

   _____

   b. There is one more possible way. Discuss with a partner how you can work it out. Draw the rows here.

   c. Rosa used squared paper to solve this problem. How can you solve this problem if you don't have squared paper? With your partner, think of another way.

Seeds and rows

2 Leon has 24 seeds.

a Draw two different ways that he can plant the seeds in equal rows.

Each row must have more than 5 seeds and fewer than 10.

b Compare your drawings with a partner. Are they the same or different?

59

Let's reason …

1 Veli has 4 packets of seeds – sunflower, tomato, green bean and pumpkin. He chooses 2 packets to plant now. He saves 2 packets to plant next month.

> You can colour blocks or cut out different shapes to show each kind of seed.

How many different pairs can he choose to plant now?

This is how Veli worked it out:

a Show 3 other pairs Veli can choose.

b How can you check if there are any other possible pairs? Discuss this with a partner.

Choosing what to plant

2 Amina also has 4 packets of seeds. She decides to plant 3 packets of seeds now, and save 1 packet to plant next month.

She draws this table to show all the **combinations** of seeds she can choose.

	🌻	🍅	🌶	🎃
	X			
		X		
			X	
				X

a Complete the sentence.

There are _____ different combinations.

b Use the letters S, T, GB and P to show the possible combinations.

Plant _____, _____ and _____ now and save _____.

Plant _____, _____ and _____ now and save _____.

Plant _____, _____ and _____ now and save _____.

Plant _____, _____ and _____ now and save _____.

3 A pumpkin plant produces about 3 or 4 pumpkins. Amina wants to grow 20 pumpkins. She asks her friends how many pumpkin plants she needs. They give these answers.

Five because
5 × 4 = 20

Six because
6 × 4 = 24

Seven because
7 × 3 = 21 and 7 × 4 = 28

a Use counters or beans to check their calculations.

b Explain which answer makes most sense to you. Tell you partner why you chose this answer.

Think, talk, write

1. These students drew a table to record when they watered their plants. Wenxi and Zola forgot to tick the table. Each column shows 1 day of the week.

🎃	Sun	Mon	Tue	Wed	Thu	Fri	Sat
Jabu		✓		✓	✓		✓
Wenxi							
Zola							

a Use the clues below to complete the table.

All the students watered the plants on 4 days.

Everyone watered their plants on Monday.

Only one of Zola's watering days was the same as Jabu's.

Jabu watered for two days in a row.

Wenxi did not water on days that contain the letter t.

b Circle the clue that gave you unnecessary information.
Explain why you did not need this clue.

> Unnecessary information is information that you do not need.

_____

_____

c Put the other clues in the order you used them.
Write 1st, 2nd, 3rd and 4th next to the clues.

d Explain to a partner why you had to use the clues in that order.

Plants need water

The students have these containers for watering plants.

cup   bottle holds 4 cups   watering can holds 5 cups   yellow bucket holds 8 cups   black bucket holds 10 cups

2 Work with a partner. Write the missing numbers in these number sentences. The first one is done for you.

a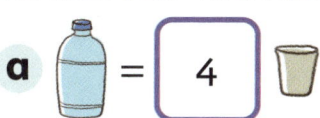

1 full bottle is **equal** to 4 cups

b

1 full watering can

c

1 full black bucket

d

e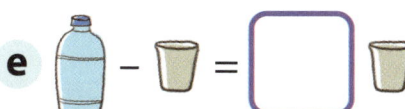

f

3 How many cups of water is it equal to?

a a half-full bottle

b a half-full yellow bucket

c a half-full black bucket

Let's solve …

1. Aisha uses her **handspan** to measure rows in her vegetable garden.

   Each row is 12 handspans long. Aisha needs to space the plants like this.

   3 handspans between sunflower plants

   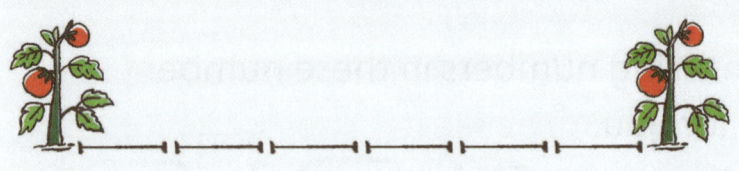
   6 handspans between tomato plants

   1 handspan between green bean plants.

   How many plants can Aisha put in each row? Draw pictures to help you work it out.

   > You can put a plant at the beginning and end of each row.

   sunflower plants　　　　　　　_____ in a row

   tomato plants　　　　　　　_____ in a row

   green bean plants　　　　　　　_____ in a row

Measuring in the garden

Think, talk, solve

Gardeners often use companion planting. They plant different plants together because the plants help each other to grow.

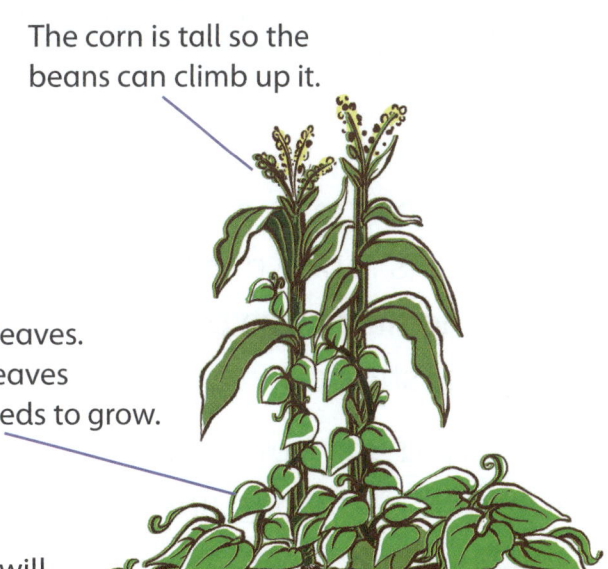

The corn is tall so the beans can climb up it.

The squash has large leaves. The shade under the leaves makes it harder for weeds to grow.

The beans help to feed the soil. This will help plants to grow next year.

2 Lyam has 9 corn plants, 15 bean plants and 12 squash plants.

His garden has three rows.

Draw a planting plan for Lyam's garden. Follow these rules:

- the same number of plants in each row
- at least 6 handspans between corn plants
- at least 1 handspan between bean plants
- at least 2 handspans between squash plants.

⊢—⊣ = 1 handspan

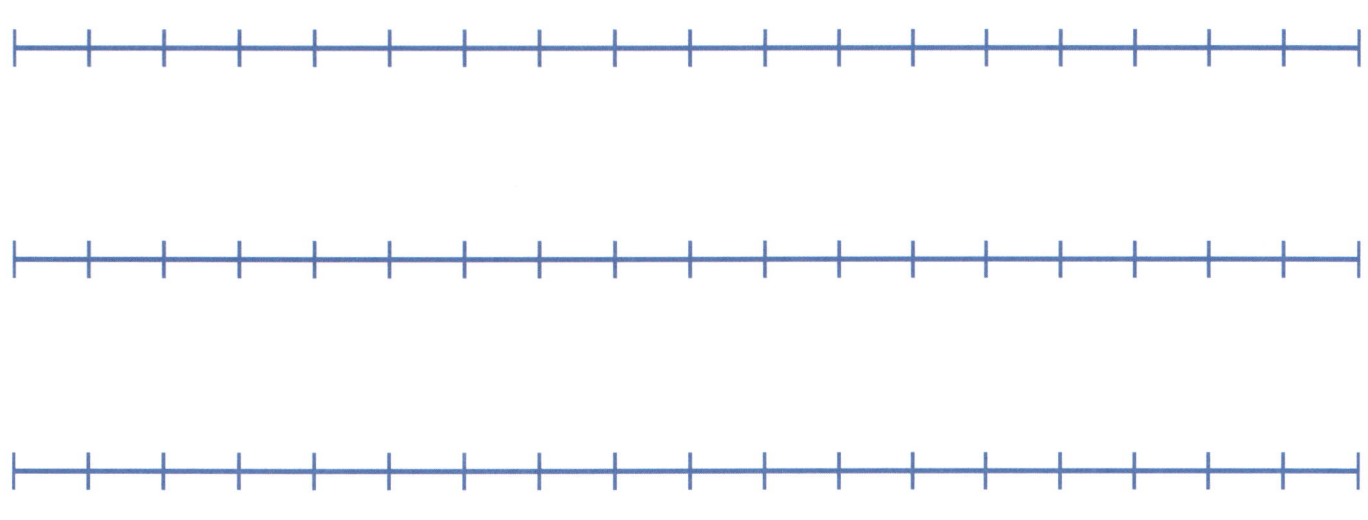

➡ Turn back to page 4 and complete the problem-solving record.

6 Exploring patterns and shapes

Let's solve …

A **mosaic** is made from small tiles. This mosaic is made of **square** tiles. Some of the tiles have been cut to make other shapes.

1 Reza and Sami are making mosaics. Draw <u>one</u> line on each square tile to make these shapes.

a 2 rectangles the same size

b 2 triangles the same size

c 1 thin rectangle and 1 thick rectangle

d 1 triangle and a shape with 4 sides (not a square)

Mosaics

2 Draw two lines on each square tile to make these shapes.

a 3 triangles of different sizes

b 4 squares

c 4 rectangles

d 2 triangles and 1 rectangle

e 3 rectangles

f 4 triangles

Think, talk, write

A square has 4 sides that are equal in length.

The corners are **right angles**. A right angle is also called a square corner.

square

some right angles

1 **a** Work with a partner. Talk about the squares you can see in each pattern.

b Write the letter of the pattern that does not have any squares.

A

B

C

D

Square patterns

2 a Design your own fabric pattern on this grid. Use squares and other shapes.

b Talk about your pattern with a partner. How are your patterns different? How are they the same?

69

Think and talk

In real life we see different patterns of circles and other round shapes.

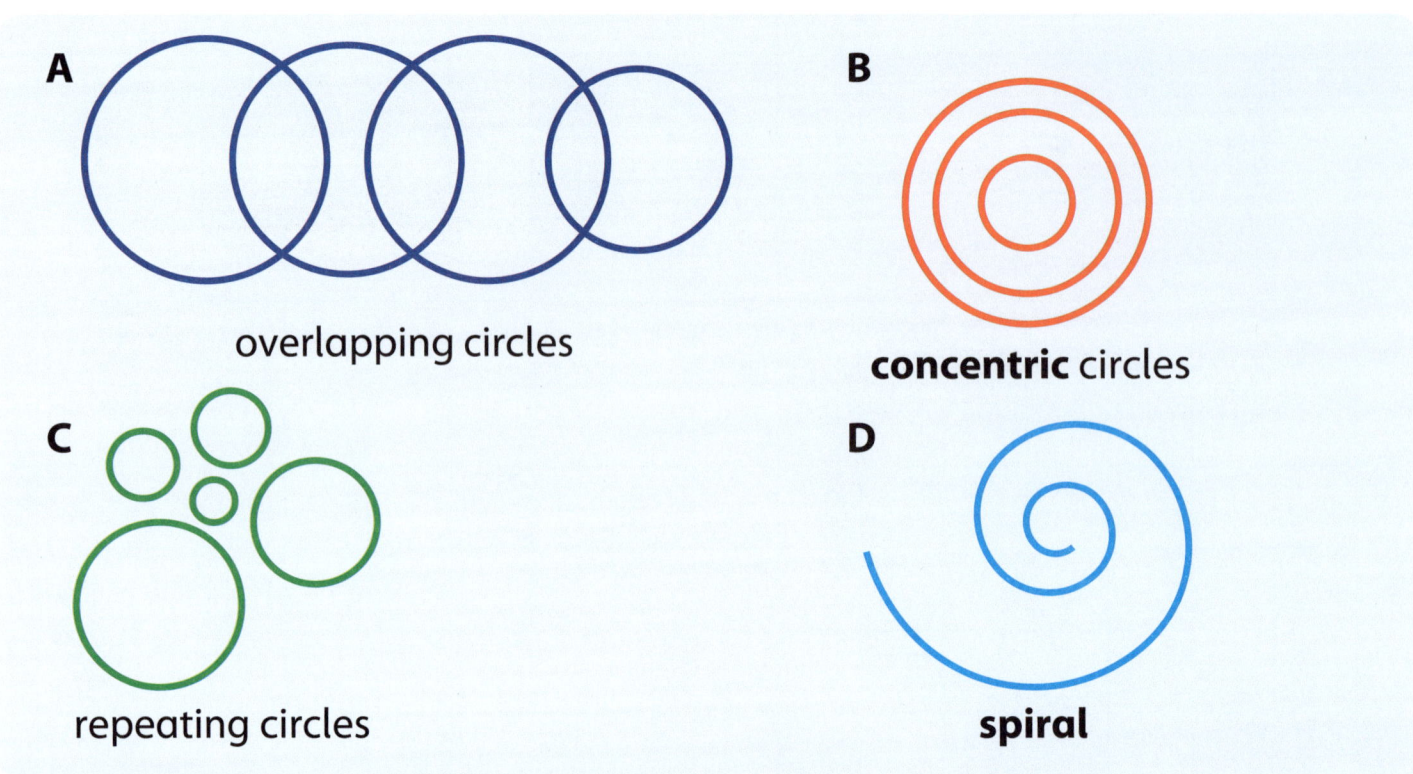

1. Describe the patterns to your partner. Use these phrases to help you.

   Circles that touch each other

   Circles inside each other, all with the same centre

   Lots of separate circles in different sizes

   A line that starts at the centre and curls round and round

2. Draw a different circle pattern in each box.

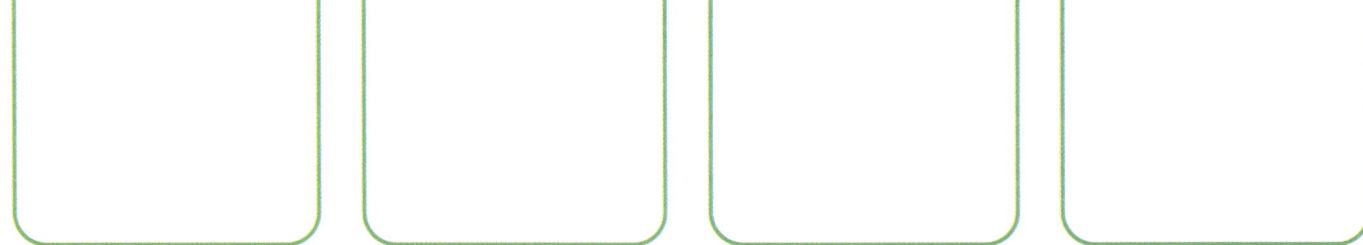

Circles and other round shapes

3 Look at these photos from real life. Decide which pattern from page 70 matches each picture best. Write A, B, C or D next to each photo.

1 Mrs Klein decorates cakes for her bakery. Today she has a lot of customers. She doesn't have time to finish decorating the cakes.

a Next to each cake, draw the shapes Mrs Klein used to decorate the cake.

b Draw the shapes to finish decorating each cake.

Decorate the cakes

2 a Decide how you would like to decorate these cakes.

- Choose the shapes for your pattern.
- Decide the rule you will use to make the pattern.
- Decorate the cake.

b Show your cakes to a partner. Can they work out the rules you used?

Let's reason ...

Number patterns follow a rule. Ask yourself ....
- What is the first number?
- Do the numbers repeat?
- Do I add or subtract to get to the next number?
- What else could I try?

1 Work out the rule. Write the missing numbers in each pattern.

a | 2 | 4 | 6 | 8 | ☐ | ☐ | ☐ |

Start at ☐. To get to the next number, _____.

b | 11 | 13 | 15 | ☐ | ☐ | ☐ | 23 |

Start at ☐. To get to the next number, _____.

c | 60 | ☐ | ☐ | 30 | 20 | 10 |

Start at ☐. To get to the next number, _____.

2 Two students used stamps to make number patterns on **100 charts**. Look at these pieces from each chart. Can you work out the students' patterns?

a
12	13	14	15	16
22	23	24	25	26
32	33	32	35	36

b
22	23	24	25
32	33	34	35
42	43	44	45
52	53	54	55

Number patterns

3 a Choose three colours. Shade the boxes to show your colours.

Colour 1 ☐   Colour 2 ☐   Colour 3 ☐

b Follow the rules in the table to colour squares on the 100 chart.

1	2	3	4	5	6	7	8	9	10
11	12	13	14	15	16	17	18	19	20
21	22	23	24	25	26	27	28	29	30
31	32	33	34	35	36	37	38	39	40
41	42	43	44	45	46	47	48	49	50
51	52	53	54	55	56	57	58	59	60
61	62	63	64	65	66	67	68	69	70
71	72	73	74	75	76	77	78	79	80
81	82	83	84	85	86	87	88	89	90
91	92	93	94	95	96	97	98	99	100

Colour	Start at number	Rule to get to the next term	Total number of terms to colour
Colour 1	43	add 10	6
Colour 3	44	add 1	4
Colour 2	42	subtract 9	4
Colour 1	48	add 10	6
Colour 2	16	add 11	4

c What shape have you made on the chart? _____

These shapes have line symmetry. They are **symmetrical**.

You can draw a line through the shape and each side is a **mirror image** of the other side.

1. Draw the line of symmetry on each shape.

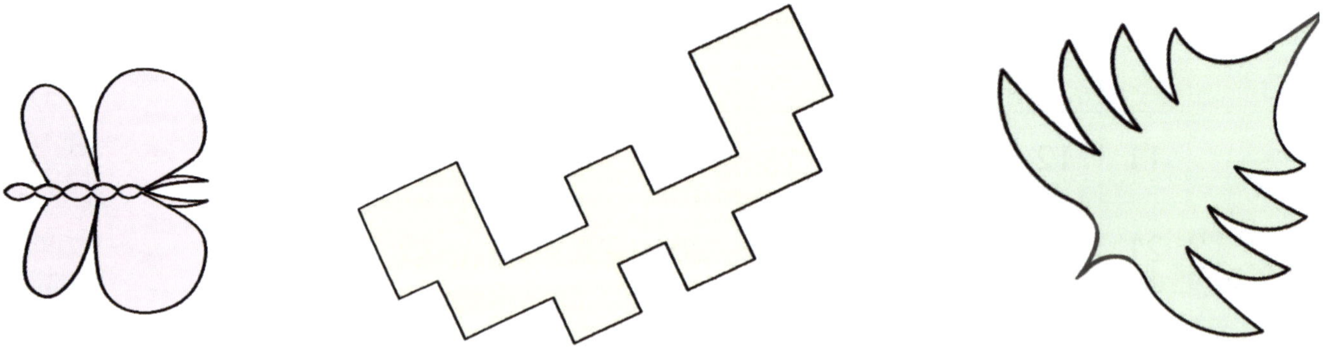

2. Make your own symmetrical patterns in each shape. Stick or draw shapes, or use pattern blocks.

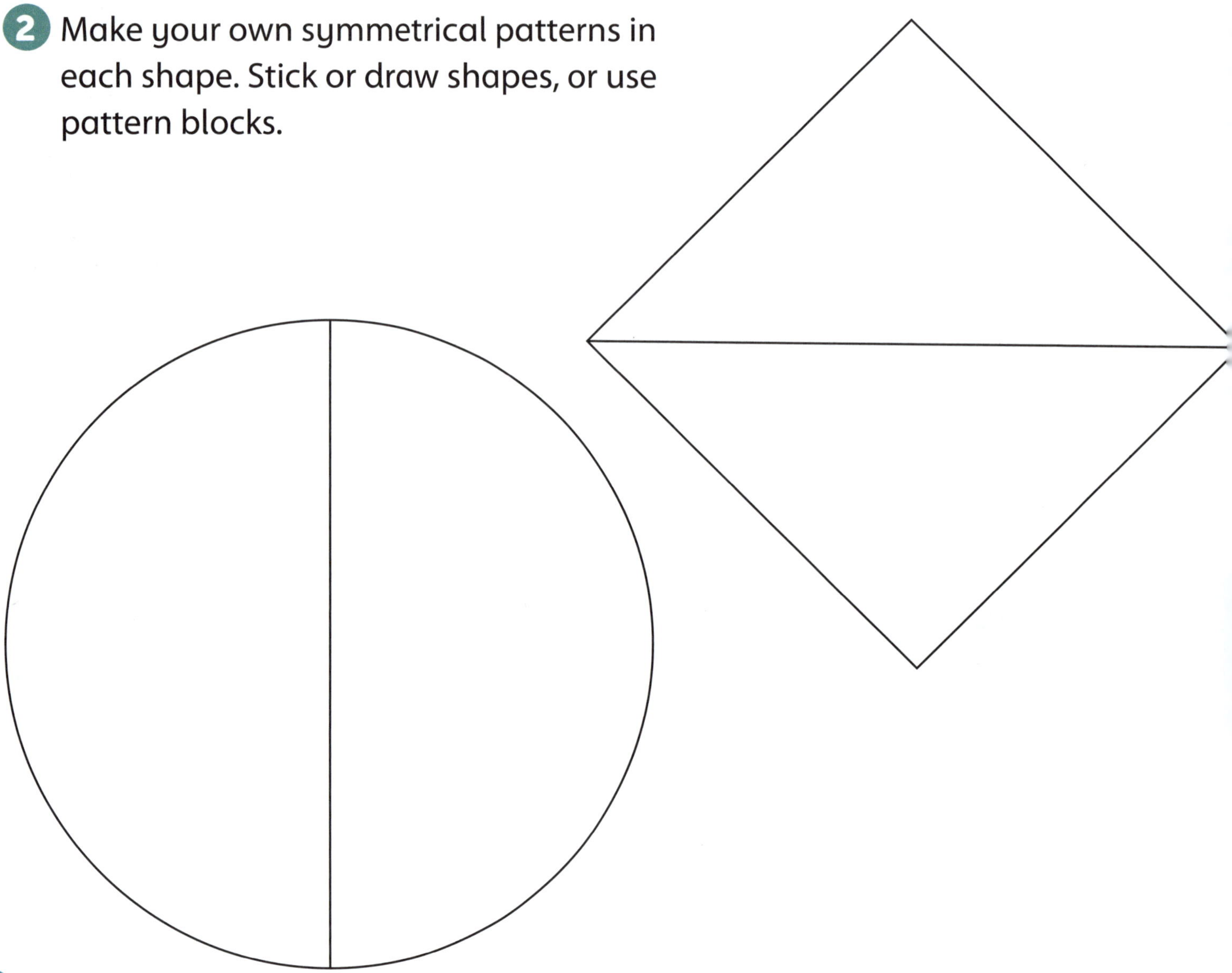

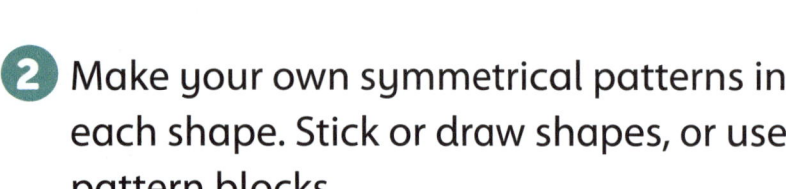

Symmetrical patterns

3 Complete these symmetrical shapes. Draw the other half of each shape.

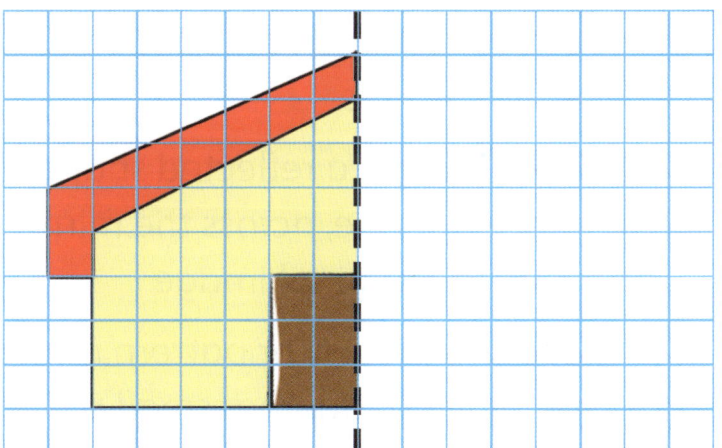 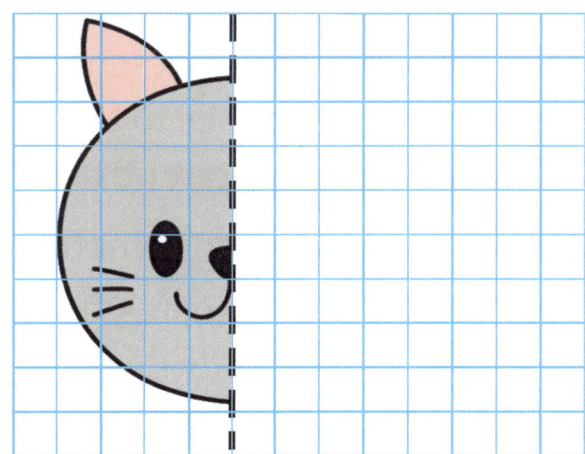

4 Only one leaf is symmetrical in each pair. Circle the symmetrical leaf.

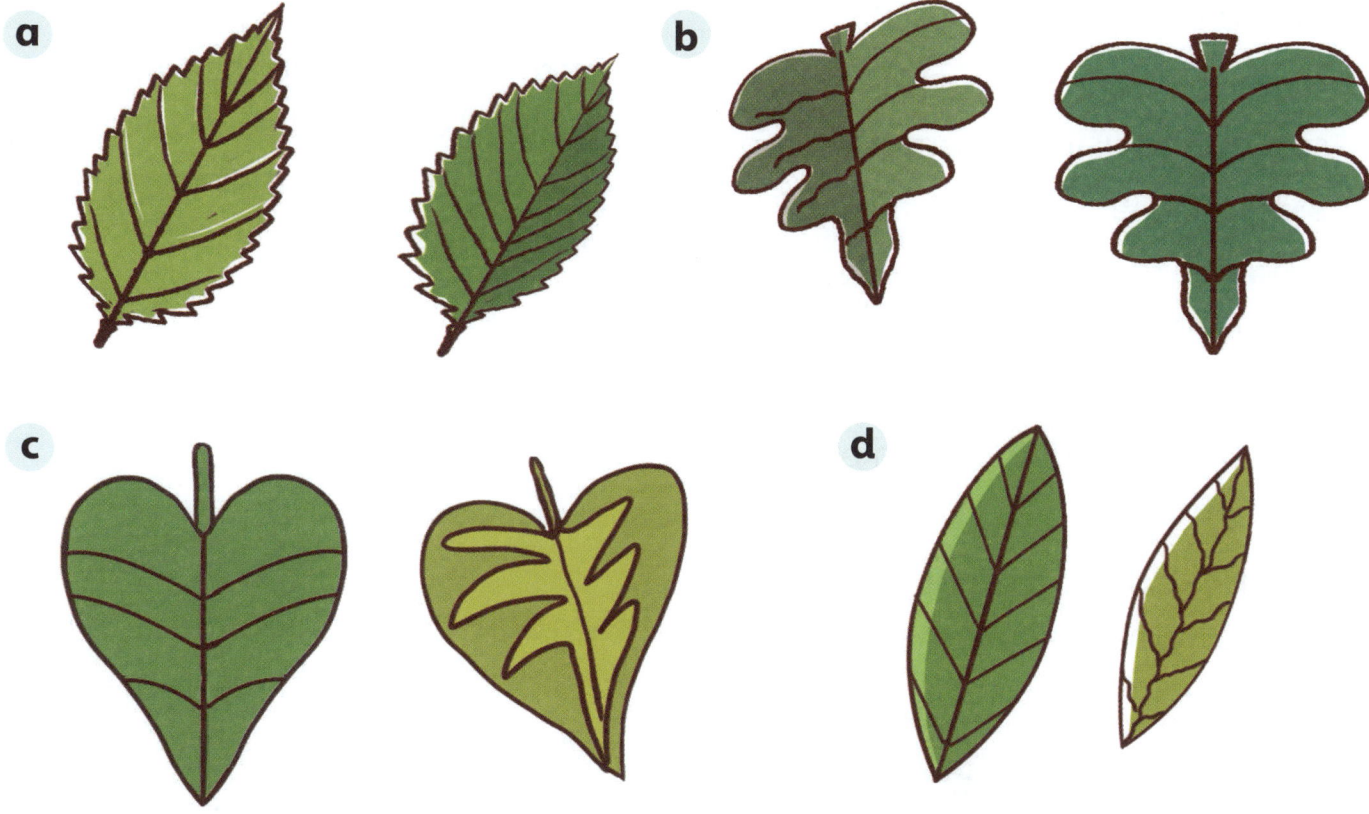

➡ Turn back to page 4 and complete the problem-solving record.

77

Glossary

General terms

around a movement describing something that goes to the side of another object to get past it

birds-eye view when something is seen from above, as if you are a bird looking down at it

change the money you get back when you pay for something with more money than it costs

combination two or more things joined together

deduce to work out the answer to something using information that you already know

eliminate to remove or get rid of something

fire exit a way out of a building in the event of a fire (if the main exit is cut off by the fire)

half-price sale an event in a shop where items are half the cost of their full price

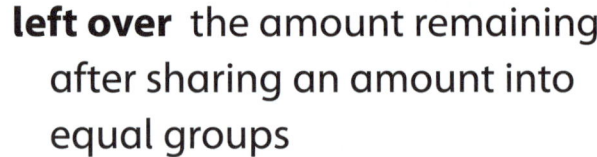

left over the amount remaining after sharing an amount into equal groups

mirror image a reflected shape, or flipped shape, across the mirror line from the original image

mosaic a picture or pattern made by placing together small pieces of glass, stone, or tiles

over a movement describing something that goes above another object to get past it

spiral a curved line that winds around a central point, with each curve getting further away from the centre

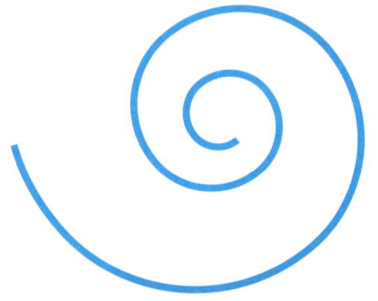

through a movement describing something that goes from one end of an object to the other

under a movement describing something that goes below another object to get past it

Mathematics terms

100 chart a chart of 100 numbers, presented in ten rows and ten columns

bar model a visual way of representing a number problem that uses horizontal bars for each of the numbers in the problem

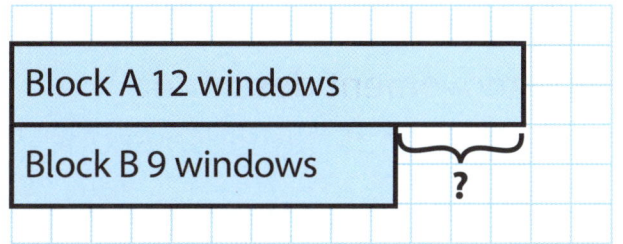

concentric a pattern of different-sized circles that all have the same centre

even number any number that is divisible by 2

handspan the width of an outstretched hand from the tip of the thumb to the tip of the little finger, used as a non-standard unit of measurement

number pattern a sequence of numbers that follow a rule

odd number any number that is not divisible by 2

right angle an angle where two lines meet to form an 'L' shape, for example, in a square or a rectangle there are 4 right angles

skip counting counting on or back in steps of the same size, for example, skip counting in 5s: 0, 5, 10, 15, 20 …

symmetrical a shape or object that has a mirror line / line of symmetry

tally table a way of recording data from an experiment or survey using tally marks in a table